Legend

nd & map

– ← – – –	Walk route	**P**	Car park
••••••••	Optional walk route	≋≋	Cliff
– – – – – –	Adjoining footpath		Rock outcrop
– · – · – · –	County boundary		Beach
☀	Viewpoint	♠ ♧	Woodland
▲ 392	Spot height		Parkland
	Built-up area	†	Church, cathedral, chapel
●	Place of interest	**WC**	Toilet
△	Steep section	🪑	Picnic area

Gloucestershire locator map

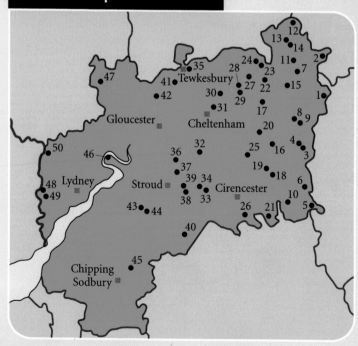

Tewkesbury

Gloucester

Cheltenham

Stroud

Cirencester

Lydney

Chipping
Sodbury

Contents

Contents

Rating: Each walk is rated for its relative difficulty compared to the other walks in this book. Walks marked 🏃 🏃 🏃 are likely to be shorter and easier with little total ascent. The hardest walks are marked 🏃 🏃 🏃 .

Walking in Safety: For advice and safety tips ➤ 128.

Introducing Gloucestershire

Gloucestershire has almost everything to make it a delightful county for discovering on foot. Within its boundaries are exceptionally varied landscapes. The Cotswolds, a region of gentle hills, valleys and gem-like villages, roll through the county. To their west is the Severn Plain, watered by Britain's longest river, and characterised by orchards and farms marked out by hedgerows that blaze with mayflower in the spring. Beyond the Severn are the Forest of Dean and the Wye Valley, border country, a distinctive mix of Celtic and Anglo-Saxon traditions. All of these have been an inspiration to some of England's finest writers and composers. Together, they combine to create a notion of mellow rosiness that epitomises rural southern England.

Gloucestershire doesn't have any real mountains: this is not a rugged county and will not suit the seekers of wilderness and rocky grandeur. The hills, though there are plenty of them, rise no higher than about 1,000ft (305m). What you do get from these hills, however, is a particular intimacy with the countryside. Climb out of Stanton, for example, and the views behind you, westward across the vale towards the Malverns and the Forest of Dean, are spectacular but never dizzy. Below you are fields of poppies and strings of golden villages, but you are never high enough to be isolated from their warmth.

What Gloucestershire lacks in rock it makes up for with an abundance of stone. Best known is the limestone of the Cotswolds, much of it a golden hue, which gives the villages of the region their widely admired charm. But there are also the standing stones of the Forest of Dean and the fossils in the Severn mud. Stone walls are everywhere on the hills and, even on the vale, stone has found its way into the fabric of some fine buildings, from churches to tithe barns.

In Gloucestershire you are never far away from tangible remains of the past. There is something remarkable to see and touch from almost every era of British history, right up to our own time. Neolithic burial chambers are widespread, and so too are the remains of Roman villas, many of which retain the fine mosaic work produced by Cirencester workshops. There are several examples of Saxon building, including a chapel amazingly still intact, an array of medieval manor houses, and hundreds of villages visually unchanged for five centuries. In the Stroud valleys abandoned mills and canals are the mark left by the Industrial Revolution.

PUBLIC TRANSPORT ⓘ

The main railway stations in the Cotswolds are Stroud, Cheltenham and Moreton-in-Marsh, all of which are served directly from London's Paddington Station. There is also a line running along the west bank of the Severn. Cheltenham is well located for trains serving the North and the South West. There are direct coaches from London Victoria and Heathrow. For local buses ring 01452 425610.

Gloucestershire has always been known for its abbeys, but most of them have disappeared or lie in ruins. However, few counties can equal the churches that remain. These are many and diverse, from the 'wool' churches in Chipping Campden and Northleach, to the cathedral at Gloucester, the abbey church at Tewkesbury or remote St Mary's, standing alone near Dymock.

If there is a shortage of anything in Gloucestershire, it is of castles. Well, you can't have it all; and yet even so, there are a couple of them. There is Sudeley Castle, where Catherine Parr is buried and, if you want the real medieval article, there is Berkeley, down on the vale.

Battles, with the exception of that at Tewkesbury, were usually fought elsewhere, leaving Gloucestershire to carry on being beautiful. I think that is what makes walking here a singular experience. Gloucestershire's natural advantages have been made use of but never transformed into something ugly – on the contrary, people and nature have got together and created something that suits them both.

Using this Book

Information panels

An information panel for each walk shows its relative difficulty (➤ 5), the distance and total amount of ascent. An indication of the gradients you will encounter is shown by the rating ▲▲ ▲▲ ▲▲ (no steep slopes) to ▲▲ ▲▲ ▲▲ (several very steep slopes).

Maps

There are 30 maps, covering 40 of the walks. Some walks have a suggested option in the same area. The information panel for these walks will tell you how much extra walking is involved. On short-cut suggestions the panel will tell you the total distance if you set out from the start of the main walk. Where an option returns to the same point on the main walk, just the distance of the loop is given. Where an option leaves the main walk at one point and returns to it at another, then the distance shown is for the whole walk. The minimum time suggested is for reasonably fit walkers and doesn't allow for stops. Each walk has a suggested map. Laminated aqua3 maps are longer lasting and water resistant.

Start Points

The start of each walk is given as a six-figure grid reference prefixed by two letters indicating which 100km square of the National Grid it refers to. You'll find more information on grid references on most Ordnance Survey maps.

Dogs

We have tried to give dog owners useful advice about how dog friendly each walk is. Please respect other countryside users. Keep your dog under control, especially around livestock, and obey local bylaws and other dog control notices.

Car Parking

Many of the car parks suggested are public, but occasionally you may find you have to park on the roadside or in a lay-by. Please be considerate when you leave your car, ensuring that access roads or gates are not blocked and that other vehicles can pass safely.

Empires and Poets at Adlestrop and Daylesford

A walk embracing the legacies of the imperialist Warren Hastings and the poet Edward Thomas.

•DISTANCE•	5 miles (8km)
•MINIMUM TIME•	2hrs
•ASCENT / GRADIENT•	230ft (70m) ▲▲ ▲ ▲
•LEVEL OF DIFFICULTY•	🚶 🚶 🚶
•PATHS•	Track, field and road, 6 stiles
•LANDSCAPE•	Rolling fields, woodland and villages
•SUGGESTED MAP•	aqua3 OS Outdoor Leisure 45 The Cotswolds
•START / FINISH•	Grid reference: SP 241272
•DOG FRIENDLINESS•	Some livestock but some open areas and quiet lanes
•PARKING•	Car park (donations requested) outside village hall
•PUBLIC TOILETS•	None on route

BACKGROUND TO THE WALK

Warren Hastings is a name that is simultaneously familiar and elusive; his role, however, in the making of the British Empire, was paramount. Born in the nearby village of Churchill, in 1732, he spent much of his childhood in Daylesford, where his grandfather was rector. When debt forced the sale of the manor, Hastings was sent to London to train for a career in commerce. He joined the East India Company, which was de facto ruler of India, and by 1773 he had attained the rank of Governor-General of Bengal, with the specific remit of cleaning up the corruption that was rife among the British and Indian ruling classes. His draconian methods were often resented but his determination and guile were effective. That India became the fulcrum of the British Empire was largely due to his work. Upon his return to England, he used his savings to repurchase Daylesford, where he died in 1818. The years before his death were bitter. A change in attitude to colonialist methods meant that Hastings was impeached for corruption. The seven year trial bankrupted him and ruined his health, although he was eventually vindicated and made Privy Councillor to George III.

Spacious Parkland

Daylesford House was rebuilt by Warren Hastings to the design of the architect Samuel Cockerell, who had been a colleague of Hastings at the East India Company. The building is in a classical style with Moorish features. The parkland around Daylesford House was laid out in 1787 by the landscape gardener Humphrey Repton in the spacious style of the day, made popular by Lancelot 'Capability' Brown. The village grew largely out of a need for cottages to house the workers who helped to make the estate profitable. Similarly, Daylesford church was rebuilt by Hastings in 1816 as a place of worship for the estate workers. By 1860 the congregation had outgrown the church, so it was redesigned to accommodate it. Inside there are monuments to the Hastings family, whilst the tomb of Warren Hastings himself lies outside the east window.

If Hastings represents the British Empire at its strongest then, in Adelstrop, you will find echoes of the changing world which signalled its decline. This small village, so characteristic of rural southern England, has come to be associated with one of the best-known poems in English, written by the war poet, Edward Thomas (1878–1917). Called simply *Adlestrop*, the poem captures a single moment as a train halts briefly at the village's station. Its haunting evocation of the drowsy silence of a hot summer day is all the more poignant when it is borne in mind that Thomas was killed by an exploding shell at Ronville near Arras in April 1917. Though trains still run on the line, the station was closed in 1964. You'll find the old station sign now decorates a bus shelter and the old staion bench has the poem inscribed upon it.

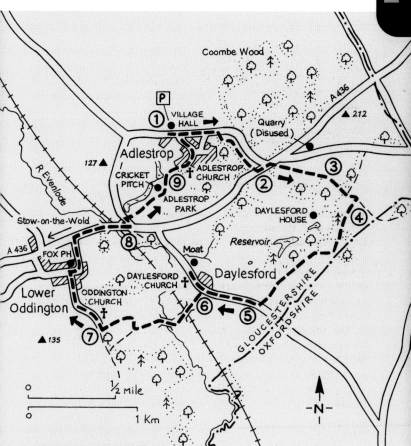

Walk 1 Directions

① From the car park turn left along the road. Pass a road on the right, the **bus shelter** bearing the Adlestrop sign, and some houses. Some 200yds (183m) after another road, turn right over a stile. Follow a woodland path to the left. Continue on this path until it meets a stile at a road.

② Cross the road with care and turn left along the verge. Before a road on the right, turn right through a gate on to a path in the **Daylesford Estate**. The path curves left towards a fence. Stay to the left of the fence until you reach a stile. Go over and cross the paddock. Pass through a gate, turn right and then left between fences.

③ Cross a bridge and follow a tree-lined avenue towards buildings. Traverse the farmyard and then turn right, passing the **estate office**.

> **WHERE TO EAT AND DRINK** ℹ
>
> The **Fox** in Lower Oddington is very homely. There is also the **Horse and Groom** in the sibling village of Upper Oddington. Stow-on-the-Wold, a short drive to the west, has many and varied pubs, restaurants and tea rooms.

④ Walk along the drive between paddocks, soon following the estate wall. Pass the gateway to the garden offices and then, as it goes sharp right, stay on this drive, eventually coming to a road. Turn right.

⑤ Walk along the road, with the estate on your right, until you come to **Daylesford estate village**. Opposite the drive to Daylesford House is a shaded footpath leading to **Daylesford church**. After visiting the church, return to the road, turn right and retrace your steps. Before the pavement ends, turn right over a stile.

> **WHILE YOU'RE THERE** ℹ
>
> **Bledington church**, about 3 miles (4.8km) south of the Oddingtons, contains an outstanding series of Perpendicular windows of beautiful, medieval stained glass. North of Adlestrop is the handsome Stuart manor house of **Chastleton**, Stow-on-the-Wold's **Toy Museum** will delight children and probably adults, too; Stow also has a set of stocks and several antique shops.

> **WHAT TO LOOK FOR** ℹ
>
> As you walk around **Daylesford Park**, try to catch a glimpse of the house – it's almost impossible as it's very cleverly concealed behind ornamental parkland. This it seems was a deliberate ruse, fashionable in the 18th century, to preserve privacy whilst creating a harmonious landscape in keeping with the surrounding countryside. In Adlestrop, look out for the site of the old **station**, immortalised by Edward Thomas.

⑥ Cross this field to a railway footbridge. Go over it and straight ahead into a field (not the field on the left) then head, bearing slightly right, for another footbridge. Cross into a field, turn right and then left at the corner. Follow the grassy field margin as it passes into another field. At the next corner, enter the field in front of you. Turn right and then left. At the next corner, go right to a track.

⑦ Turn right and pass **Oddington church**. Continue to a junction in the village and turn right. Pass the **Fox** pub and continue to another junction. Turn right and walk along the pavement. Where this ends, cross the road carefully to the pavement opposite.

⑧ Beyond the bridge, turn left along the **Adlestrop road** and turn immediately right over two stiles. Walk towards **Adlestrop Park**. As you draw level with the cricket pitch go diagonally left to a gate about 100yds (91m) to the right of the pavilion.

⑨ Follow the track past **Adlestrop church**. At the next junction turn left through the village until you reach the **bus stop**. Turn left here to return to the car park at the start of the walk.

The Lost Villages of the Ditchfords

A walk among the ghosts of former medieval agricultural communities, abandoned since the 15th century.

•DISTANCE•	5 miles (8km)
•MINIMUM TIME•	1hr 45min
•ASCENT / GRADIENT•	130ft (40m) ▲▲ ▲
•LEVEL OF DIFFICULTY•	🚶🚶 🚶🚶 🚶🚶
•PATHS•	Track and field, quiet lanes, ford or bridge, 2 stiles
•LANDSCAPE•	Rolling fields, with good views at some points
•SUGGESTED MAP•	aqua3 OS Outdoor Leisure 45 The Cotswolds
•START / FINISH•	Grid reference: SP 240362
•DOG FRIENDLINESS•	Some livestock and some not very encouraging signs
•PARKING•	Lay-bys on Todenham's main street, south of village hall
•PUBLIC TOILETS•	None on route

BACKGROUND TO THE WALK

There are cases of so-called 'lost villages' all over England and almost as many theories and explanations for their demise. The principal culprit is often said to be the Black Death, sweeping through the countryside in the 14th century and emptying villages of their inhabitants. However, this is by no means the only possibility and in the case of the Ditchfords there do appear to be other reasons for their disappearance. Ditchford is a name that was widespread in this area (perhaps because of their proximity to the Fosse Way – 'fosse' meaning ditch in Old English). Remnants of this, in the form of the names of houses and farms, are still evident on detailed maps, but of the three villages – Ditchford Frary, Lower Ditchford and Upper Ditchford – there is almost no trace.

Abandonment

A 15th-century witness, a priest from Warwickshire called John Rouse, wrote in 1491 that the Ditchfords had been abandoned during his lifetime. Changes in agricultural practices are thought to be the principal reason for this abandonment. As farming gradually became more efficient there was a disinclination to cultivate the stony soils of the more exposed and windswept upland areas.

At the same time, in the Cotswolds, the wool trade was rapidly supplanting arable farming, as the wolds were given over to sheep farming. Much of the land was owned by the great abbeys who, deriving a third of their income from wool, turned vast tracts of land over to summer pasture in the uplands and winter pastures on the more sheltered lower slopes. The result was, of course, that the villagers, mostly farm labourers who had for centuries depended on access to arable land for their livelihood, lost that access. They simply had to move elsewhere in search of work.

Today there are no solid remains of any of the three villages. What you can see, however, is a series of regular rolls and shapes in the land that indicate settlement. Upper Ditchford, which stood on the slope near Neighbrook Farm, is the least obvious but you can see banked enclosures and terraces that probably supported buildings. The site is somewhat clearer in the case of Lower Ditchford, where there are terraces and the site of a manor house and moat. Ditchford Frary has left its name to a nearby farmhouse.

Surviving Village

Todenham survived the rigours of depopluation, and today is a quiet and unspoilt village on the edge of the Cotswolds. It's really a long, single road flanked by an assortment of houses and their leafy gardens. The manor house dates from the end of the Georgian period whilst the church is worth a visit for its decorated and Perpendicular interior. Its features include a 13th-century font with the names of 18th-century churchwardens inscribed upon it.

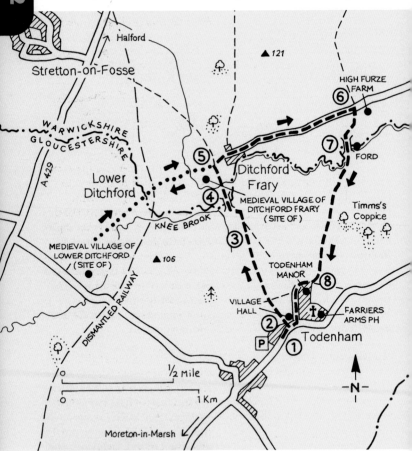

Walk 2 Directions

① From a lay-by below **Todenham village hall** walk up towards the hall and turn left just before it, along a track that runs to the right of a house.

② After a few paces go right up a bank to a gate. Pass into a field and head straight across. Go through another gate on the far side, into a field of undulations indicating medieval ploughing. Continue on the same line to a stile – cross into the neighbouring field and, staying

Walk 2

WHILE YOU'RE THERE ⓘ
Tuesday is **market day** in Moreton-in-Marsh; it's the largest, indeed practically the only, weekly market left in the Cotswolds. Full of bustling bargain hunters, it gives a hint, at least, of how village life must have once been.

on its upper part, go straight ahead, in the general direction of a large house.

③ Cross another stile and soon join a farm track. Where the track goes into a field on the right, go straight ahead. At the bottom of the field the path may become indistinct – look for a small bridge, with gates at either end, amid the undergrowth 50yds (46m) to your left.

④ Cross this bridge and then go straight ahead, crossing a field (the site of **Ditchford Frary**) with a farmhouse before you to the right. On the other side go through a gate, cross another field and pass through a gate to a farm track.

⑤ If you wish to see the site of **Lower Ditchford**, turn left here and keep going over the former railway line until you approach a road – the

remains are to your left. Then return along the track. Otherwise turn right on the track and pass behind the farmhouse. The track becomes a metalled lane.

⑥ Just before **High Furze Farm** turn right through a gate into a field. Follow its left margin until it dips down to a ford across Knee Brook. Turn right here and after a few paces find a bridge on your left.

⑦ Cross this and then return to the faint, grassy track that rises from the ford. By staying on this line, with the brook now to your right, you will come to a gate in the top corner. Go through on to a track that rises between two high hedges. Parts of this may be boggy but soon the track will become firmer and will eventually carry you to a junction opposite an entrance to **Todenham Manor**.

⑧ Turn right here and follow this track as it curves left, around the manor, and finally brings you back to the village with the **village hall** on your right. Turn left for the **church** and the **Farriers Arms** pub, right to return to your car.

WHERE TO EAT AND DRINK ⓘ
The highly attractive **Farriers Arms** is in Todenham, a short way up from the church. The market town of Moreton-in-Marsh, 3 miles (4.8km) south west, has plenty of pubs, cafes, and restaurants, including the well-known **Marsh Goose**.

WHAT TO LOOK FOR ⓘ
As you are crossing the fields at the beginning of the walk, look out for the pleats in the fields that indicate **medieval ridge and furrow** ploughing techniques. These are common all over central England, though many have been ploughed out by modern machinery. The furrows were created by cumbersome ox-drawn ploughs, the ridges separated different farmers' workings in the same open field. Each furrow would originally have been about a furlong (201m) in length, the distance being about as far as the ploughing beast could pull before it needed a rest.

Windrush Stone Secrets

An insight into Cotswold stone, the building blocks of the region's beauty.

•DISTANCE•	6 miles (9.7km)
•MINIMUM TIME•	2hs 30min
•ASCENT / GRADIENT•	120ft (37m) ▲ ▲ ▲
•LEVEL OF DIFFICULTY•	🚶🚶 🚶🚶 🚶🚶
•PATHS•	Fields, tracks and pavement, 11 stiles
•LANDSCAPE•	Streams, fields, open country and villages
•SUGGESTED MAP•	aqua3 OS Outdoor Leisure 45 The Cotswolds
•START / FINISH•	Grid reference: SP 192130
•DOG FRIENDLINESS•	Some care required but long stretches without livestock
•PARKING•	Windrush village
•PUBLIC TOILETS•	None on route

BACKGROUND TO THE WALK

The Cotswolds, characterised by villages of gilded stone, lie mainly in Gloucestershire. Stone is everywhere here – walk across any field and shards of oolitic limestone lie about the surface like bits of fossilised litter. This limestone, for long an obstacle to arable farming, is a perfect building material. In the past almost every village was served by its own quarry, a few of which are still worked today. Limestone is a sedimentary rock, made largely of material derived from living organisms that thrived in the sea that once covered this part of Britain. The rock is therefore easily extracted and easily worked; some of it will actually yield to a handsaw. Of course this is something of a generalisation as, even in a small area, the quality of limestone varies considerably in colour and in texture, suiting certain uses more than others. But it is for its golden hue, due to the presence of iron oxide, that it is most famous.

The composition of the stone dictates the use to which it will be put. Some limestone, with a high proportion of grit, is best suited to wall building or to hut building. Some outcrops are in very thin layers and are known as 'presents' because they provide almost ready-made material for roof-slates. Sometimes the stone needs a little help and in this case it is left out in the winter so that frost freezes the moisture trapped between layers, forcing them apart. The stone can then be shaped into slates and hung on a wooden roof trellis by means of a simple nail. The smallest slates are placed at the top of the roof, the largest at the bottom. Because of their porous nature, they have to overlap and the roof is built at a steep pitch, so that the rain runs off quickly.

There are four basic types of stone construction in the Cotswolds – dry-stone, mortared rubble, dressed stone and ashlar. Dry-stone, without mortar, is used in boundary walls. Mortared rubble, on the other hand, depends on the use of lime pointing in order to stay upright. Dressed stone refers to the craft of chopping and axing stone to give a more polished and tighter finish. Ashlar is the finest technique, where the best stone is sawn and shaped into perfectly aligned blocks that act either as a facing on rubble, or which, more rarely, make up the entire wall. Ashlar was used in the finer houses and, occasionally, in barns. The quality of Cotswold stone has long been recognised and the quarries here, west of Burford, provided building material for St Paul's Cathedral and several Oxford colleges.

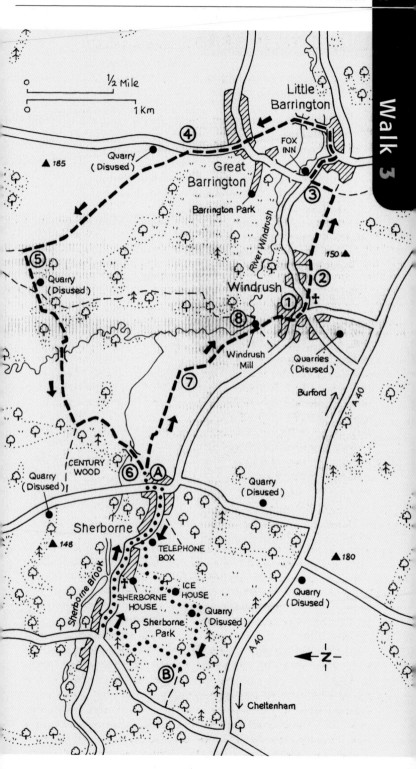

Walk 3 Directions

① Walk out of the village, keeping to the left of the church and, after about 100yds (91m), go right, through a gate into a field. Go across this field to the other side, keeping to the left.

② Go through the right-hand gate and continue across a series of stiles until you emerge in a large field at a wide grass strip (careful here, as it is used for 'galloping' horses) with the houses of **Little Barrington** opposite. Cross two thirds of the field, then turn left and head for the hedge at the bottom.

③ Go through a gap to a road. Ahead is the **Fox Inn**. Turn right, enter Little Barrington and turn left along a 'No Through Road' which narrows to a path. Where the path becomes a lane, go left across a bridge and continue, eventually emerging in **Great Barrington** at a cross. Take the road in front of you.

> ### WHAT TO LOOK FOR ⓘ
> Towards Little Barrington you should see **Barrington Park**, in the middle distance on your left. This Palladian house was built by William Kent for Earl Talbot (George II's Lord Chancellor) in the 18th century.

④ Where the wall on your left ends, go left on to a track and immediately right. Stay on this track for a little over 1 mile (1.6km) until you come to a junction of tracks with large hedges before you.

⑤ Turn left and follow this track until you enter scrubby woodland. Cross the river and follow a grassy track until, just before **Century Woods**, you turn left into a field.

Follow the margin of the woods. Cross another bridge into a field and turn half right to the far corner. Go over the bridge, cross a stile and go half left to another stile.

⑥ Take the track before you and then turn left over another stile (Point ④ on Walk 4). Cross this field to go through a gate and walk along the right-hand margin on the same line for several fields.

> ### WHERE TO EAT AND DRINK ⓘ
> En route there is one pub, the **Fox Inn**, at Little Barrington, charmingly located by a stream. In the summer you can eat in the garden, which is very helpful if you are with children.

⑦ Come to a stile at a corner. Go over into the next field and cross it on a right diagonal, in the general direction of a distant village. On the far side go through a gap into another field, with a stone wall on your right. Continue for several fields and pass a **stone barn** to the right, at which point the **River Windrush** will appear to your left. Finally, pass a tin barn to your left-hand side, just as you arrive at a gate by a lane.

⑧ Opposite, go up to a stile. In the next field follow its perimeter as it goes right and brings you to a stile. Cross to a path and follow it into **Windrush** village.

> ### WHILE YOU'RE THERE
> To the east is the small but magnificent town of **Burford** (actually in Oxfordshire). Its main street, flanked by a cascade of beautiful houses, leads down to the River Windrush, spanned by a bridge dating from 1322. Wool drove Burford's early prosperity; then, in the 18th century, it was an important stop on the coaching route to Oxford and London.

Sherborne Sheep Village

Extend Walk 3 with a visit to a sheepish estate village.
See map and information panel for Walk 3

•DISTANCE•	2¾ miles (4.4km)
•MINIMUM TIME•	1hr
•ASCENT / GRADIENT•	210ft (65m) ▲▲ ▲ ▲
•LEVEL OF DIFFICULTY•	🚶🚶 🚶 🚶

Walk 4 Directions (Walk 3 option)

The estate village of Sherborne originally belonged to Winchcombe Abbey. Huge flocks of sheep were gathered here for shearing, with much of the wool exported to Flanders and Italy. After the dissolution of the monasteries the estate was purchased by the Dutton family, who built themselves a fine house with the help of the eminent local quarryman, Valentine Strong. In the 19th century the house was rebuilt using estate stone but eventually it became a boarding school and has now been divided into luxury flats. The estate belongs to the National Trust. The village has some very pretty cottages, one of which, in the eastern part, has somehow acquired a Norman arch. From the road near the church are sweeping rustic views across Sherborne Brook and its water-meadows, where once the medieval flocks of sheep would have grazed.

From Point Ⓐ turn right over a stile, following a path between cottages to a road. Turn left then right, into **Sherborne**. Enter the Sherborne Estate through a doorway beside the telephone box and follow the main path. **Sherborne House** will appear to the right. The path bears sharp left; after 150yds (137m) turn right. After a further 150yds (137m) turn left on to another gently ascending path. Stay left of a tree surrounded by a metal seat on a mound and enter a path on the far side to head for a gate. Go through the smaller of two gates, pass the old **ice house** and head for a gate.

Follow the main path through the trees. Join another path and, at a gate, go through on to a farm track and turn right. Follow this to a gate at a farmyard, Point Ⓑ. Go through this and turn immediately right to pass through another gateway. Then pass a gate on the right and turn right into a field to follow its right-hand margin.

Follow this as it bears left at the corner and descend to the bottom corner where the path will take you into conifer woodland. Follow this wide path down until you come to a fork. Stay left and keep to the path as it skirts the woods, bearing right to flatten out at the bottom. Stay on it all the way to a doorway in a wall. Emerge at a road and turn right. Follow the pavement through the village, passing the **church** on the right, and return to Point Ⓐ.

Walk 5

Lechlade and the Thames

You are never far from the river on this route, centred on a once bustling crossroads in a quiet corner bordering Wiltshire and Oxfordshire.

•DISTANCE•	5 miles (8km)
•MINIMUM TIME•	2hrs
•ASCENT / GRADIENT•	Negligible
•LEVEL OF DIFFICULTY•	
•PATHS•	Fields, tracks and road, 8 stiles
•LANDSCAPE•	Water-meadows, river and village
•SUGGESTED MAP•	aqua3 OS Explorer 170 Abingdon
•START / FINISH•	Grid reference: SU 214995
•DOG FRIENDLINESS•	Good but many swans and ducks beside rivers
•PARKING•	Lechlade main street or square
•PUBLIC TOILETS•	On Burford Street in Lechlade

Walk 5 Directions

From the handsome **Market Square** walk west along the **High Street** and then left along **Thames Street**. Look around and you will see the high, slender spire of the majestic parish church, a constant presence throughout this walk even as the route strays into Wiltshire and Oxfordshire. The spire was perfectly described by the 16th-century writer John Leland as a 'pratie pyramis of stone'.

Halfpenny Bridge is a toll bridge that opened in 1792 – the toll house is still standing. Cross this bridge and, at the end, drop down some

steps on the right to the riverbank. Walk ahead, with the river to your right, for just over ½ mile (800m) until, immediately after a bridge across the Thames, you see an old roundhouse among the trees on the far bank. Here the River Coln joins the Thames, alongside the now silted-up Thames and Severn Canal.

Lechlade was the upper limit for navigation of the Thames. In 1789, when the Thames and Severn Canal was completed, it became possible to move cargoes from ship to barge for the 29 mile (46.5km) journey across Gloucestershire. Local stone went east and was extensively used in London and Oxford.

Continue along the riverbank, cross a footbridge over a stream and head across the field to find a stile to the left of a house. The walk continues by turning left along the lane but, if you want to visit **Inglesham church**, turn right. This charming medieval building, much admired by William Morris, contains an exceptionally beautiful 13th-century

WHAT TO LOOK FOR ⓘ

Although the attractions of **Lechlade** might seem to be confined to the main street and to the church, it is worth spending some time wandering the streets that run off from the market square. Along them are a number of handsome buildings dating from the 17th to the 19th century.

Madonna and Child. At the end of the lane turn right, along the main road (making use of the verge). After 150yds (137m) turn left towards Buscot. In ¼ mile (1.2km) turn left along the drive of **Buscot Wick Farm**. Just before the farmyard turn right along a drive before cottages and then go across some grass to a gate. Turn left around a house and after 150yds (137m) go half right across a field to a gate. In the next field stay on the same line to another gate. Go through into a field, follow a hedge and then turn left through a gate and cross a field to the road. Go through a gate on the other side, cross the field to a stile and turn left into the churchyard.

Buscot church contains a striking east window by the pre-Raphaelite artist Edward Burne-Jones, a pulpit partly made from a Flemish triptych and some delightful paintings, part of the memorials to members of the Loveden family. Leave by the lychgate and follow the riverbank to emerge at **Buscot Weir**. Here turn right if you want to visit the estate village of **Buscot**, which now belongs to the National Trust; there is a small shop and a pub on its short main street. Otherwise walk on to pass **Lock Cottage** and make your way across a succession of locks and bridges to a stile. Do not cross this but turn left to follow the **Thames Path**. Follow the river's

meanderings until it brings you to a wooden bridge. Cross this and turn right to continue along the riverbank, noting the River Leach across to your right, which joins the River Thames just before **St John's Bridge**.

With both the River Coln and the River Leach flowing into the River Thames hereabouts, it is no surprise that there are a number of bridges. (Lechlade is in fact the only Gloucestershire town on the Thames.) Beneath the bridges, crowds of river pleasure craft have replaced the trading vessels of the past while above, notwithstanding their age, the bridges continue their function, bearing the loads of modern-day road traffic.

Walk beneath **St John's Bridge**, which dates from the 14th century and which takes its name from a former nearby priory. Pass a lock, noting the statue of Father Thames that was built for the Great Exhibition of 1851 and which was moved here from its original site at Thames Head. Then enter the wide meadow ahead through a gate, the spire of Lechlade's parish church towers out of the flat landscape. The parish church was the inspiration for Percy Shelley's *Summer Evening Meditation*. Continue to the **Halfpenny Bridge** and **Lechlade**.

WHILE YOU'RE THERE ⓘ

Just over 2 miles (3.2km) to the east of Lechlade is **Kelmscot**. The poet and craftsman, William Morris, the leading light of the Arts and Crafts Movement, lived in the Elizabethan manor house here from 1871 until his death in 1896. Morris is buried in the churchyard, whilst there is a charming carving of him on the village's Memorial Cottages.

Side by Side with the Eastleaches

Two churches, just a stone's throw apart across a narrow stream, give a clue to the complicated evolution of the English parish boundary.

•DISTANCE•	4½ miles (7.2km)
•MINIMUM TIME•	1hr 45min
•ASCENT / GRADIENT•	100ft (30m) ▲▲ ▲ ▲
•LEVEL OF DIFFICULTY•	🚶🚶 🚶 🚶
•PATHS•	Tracks and lanes, valley paths and woodland, 6 stiles
•LANDSCAPE•	Villages, open wold, narrow valley and streams
•SUGGESTED MAP•	aqua3 OS Outdoor Leisure 45 The Cotswolds
•START / FINISH•	Grid reference: SP 200052
•DOG FRIENDLINESS•	Sheep country – dogs under control at all times
•PARKING•	Village of Eastleach Turville
•PUBLIC TOILETS•	None on route

BACKGROUND TO THE WALK

These two Cotswold villages, sitting cheek by jowl in a secluded valley, carry an air of quiet perfection. And yet Eastleach Turville and Eastleach Martin are quite distinctive, and each has a parish church (though one is now redundant). St Andrews in Eastleach Turville faces St Micheal and St Martin's across the narrow River Leach. Their origins lie in the development of the parish system from the early days of the Anglo-Saxon Church.

The Anglo-Saxon Kingdoms

The English parish has its origins in the shifting rivalries of Saxon England; for the one thing that united the various Saxon kingdoms was the Church. The first 'parishes' were really the Anglo-Saxon kingdoms. Christianity, the new power in the land, not only saved souls but also secured alliances. The Pope's aim was to invest more bishops to act as pastors and proselytisers, but at the same time their appointments were useful politically, helping to smooth the way as larger kingdoms absorbed their smaller neighbours. The number of appointments would also depend on local factors. Wessex, for example, was divided into shires and so a bishop was appointed for each one. Later the Normans appointed Archdeacons, whose job was to ensure that church buildings were maintained for worship. Over the centuries the assorted conventions and appointments that had accumulated through usage coalesced into a hierarchical English Church. For a long time, however, control was not tight. Missionaries, for example, would occasionally land from Ireland and found their own churches, quite independently of local potentates. Rulers and local landholders were certainly influential in the development of the parish system, but many parishes also derived from the gradual disintegration of the local 'minster', a central church on consecrated ground which controlled a group of client chapels. As population and congregations grew, the chapels themselves became new parish churches, with rights equal to those of the minster. This included the right to bury the dead in their own graveyard and administration of births and marriages.

Walk 6

Tithe Payments

With the passage of time and the establishment of a single English kingdom, the idea of a parish had diminished geographically to something akin to its modern size. By the 10th century the parish had become the accepted framework for the enforcement of the payment of tithes, the medieval eqivalent of an income tax. By the 12th century much of the modern diocesan map of England was established. So in the Eastleaches, all these developments come together and you find two parish churches virtually side by side. With politics, power and bureaucracy all playing a part, it's likely that the pastoral needs of the community were quite a long way down the list of factors which led to their creation.

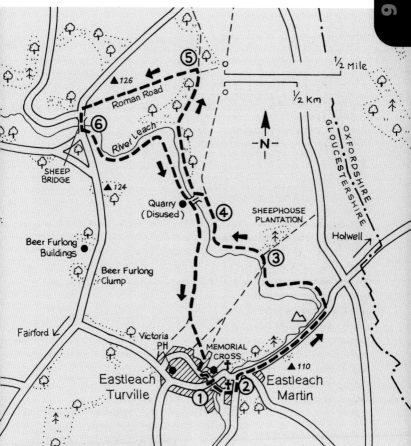

Walk 6 Directions

① From the **memorial cross** in **Eastleach Turville** walk along the road with the river on your right. After a few paces locate a path on your right to cross the **clapper bridge** and follow the path into the

churchyard of Eastleach Martin. Pass to the right of the church and emerge at a road.

② Turn left and then turn right at a junction, taking the lower road in the direction of Holwell. Walk on for perhaps 600yds (549m) to where the road begins to rise

Walk 6

steeply. Turn left here, through a gate into a field, and follow an obvious grassy track at the base of a slope for ½ mile (800m).

③ This will bring you to a corner of **Sheephouse Plantation**. Turn left and walk into a field with the woods to your right. Continue to a gate at a field – do not go through this but continue forward with the field to your right. Soon you will reach a small area of scrubby trees, turn right here over a stile into a field and turn left.

WHAT TO LOOK FOR ⓘ

The little clapper bridge linking the two parishes is known locally as **Keble's Bridge**, after a family who were eminent in the area. John Keble, after whom Keble College in Oxford is named, was nominal curate for the two parishes in the 19th century. In the middle part of the walk the straight track to a road is part of **Akeman Street**, the Roman road that linked Cirencester with St Albans.

④ Continue, passing through gates, until you come to a gated bridge on your left. Do not cross this but continue forward towards a gate at the edge of woodland. Go through and follow a woodland path until you emerge at a clearing. Walk to the other side to re-enter woodland and continue to a track.

WHILE YOU'RE THERE ⓘ

There are two places near by worth visiting while you are in the area. To the south is **Lechlade** (► Walk 5), Gloucestershire's only settlement on the River Thames. There is a handsome Market Square, an idyllic riverside and several fascinating old streets to wander through. To the west is **Fairford** (► Walk 10), a handsome village noted for its fine church containing one of the only sets of medieval stained glass in the country.

WHERE TO EAT AND DRINK ⓘ

Eastleach Turville has a lovely little pub, the **Victoria**, in the western part of the village. Nearby Southrop, to the south, also has the **Swan**, a creeper-clad old pub with real fires in winter and a wide choice of food. In Coln St Alwyns, to the west, you'll find the **New Inn**, everybody's idea of a classic Cotswold pub and serving excellent food.

⑤ Turn left here and follow a track out of the woods and across fields until you come to a road. Turn left here, cross **Sheep Bridge** and, just before a turning to the right, go left into a field.

⑥ Bear right along the valley bottom, then left and right again. This will bring you to a gate. Go through it, on to a track, and soon pass the gated bridge again. Follow the wall on your right as it curves up to a gate and then stay on the same line through gates until you emerge at a road in **Eastleach Turville**. Turn left to make your way back to the start.

The Nabob of Sezincote and Bourton-on-the-Hill

Discovering the influences of India through the Cotswold home of Sir Charles Cockerell.

•**DISTANCE**•	3 miles (4.8km)
•**MINIMUM TIME**•	1hr 15min
•**ASCENT / GRADIENT**•	85ft (25m) ▲▲▲
•**LEVEL OF DIFFICULTY**•	🚶🚶 🚶 🚶
•**PATHS**•	Tracks, fields and lanes, 7 stiles
•**LANDSCAPE**•	Hedges, field and spinney on lower part of escarpment
•**SUGGESTED MAP**•	aqua3 OS Outdoor Leisure 45 The Cotswolds
•**START / FINISH**•	Grid reference: SP 175324
•**DOG FRIENDLINESS**•	Under close control – likely to be a lot of livestock
•**PARKING**•	Street below Bourton-on-the-Hill church, parallel with main road
•**PUBLIC TOILETS**•	None on route

BACKGROUND TO THE WALK

For anyone with a fixed idea of the English country house, Sezincote will come as something of a surprise. It is, as the poet John Betjeman said, 'a good joke, but a good house, too'. Built on the plan of a typical large country house of the era, in every other respect it is thoroughly unconventional. A large copper onion dome crowns the house, whilst at each corner of the roof are finials in the form of miniature minarets. The walls are of Cotswold stone, but the Regency windows, and much of the decoration, owe a lot to Eastern influence.

Hindu Architecture

Sezincote is a reflection of the fashions of the early 19th century. Just as engravings brought back from Athens had been the inspiration for 18th-century Classicism, so the colourful aqua-tints brought to England from India by returning artists, such as William and Thomas Daniell, were a profound influence on architects and designers. Sezincote was one of the first results of this fashion and the first example of Hindu architecture in England that was actually lived in. Sir Charles Cockerell was a 'nabob', the Hindi-derived word for a European who had made their wealth in the East. On his retirement from the East India Company he had the house built by his brother, Samuel Pepys Cockerell, an architect. The eminent landscape gardener Humphry Repton helped Cockerell to choose the most picturesque elements of Hindu architecture from the Daniells' drawings.

Pavilion Inspiration

Some modern materials, like cast iron, were thought to complement the intricacies of traditional Mogul design. The garden buildings took on elements from Hindu temples, with a lotus shaped temple pool, Hindu columns supporting a bridge and the widespread presence of snakes, sacred bulls and lotus buds. The Prince of Wales was an early visitor. The experience obviously made some impression as the extemely Mogul Brighton Pavilion arose not long after. Betjeman was a regular guest at Sezincote during his undergraduate days. 'Stately and strange it stood, the nabob's house, Indian without and coolest Greek within, looking from Gloucestershire to Oxfordshire'.

Measuring Up in Bourton-on-the-Hill

This walks begins and ends in Bourton-on-the-Hill, a pretty village that would be exceptional were it not for traffic streaming through it on the A44. Nevertheless, there is quite a lot to see here. The church owes its impressive features to the fact that the village was formerly owned by Westminster Abbey, whose income was handsomely supplemented by sales of wool from their vast flocks on the surrounding hills. There is a fine 15th-century clerestory, lighting an interior notable for its substantial nave columns and a rare bell-metal Winchester Bushel and Peck (8 gallons/35.2 litres and 2 gallons/8.8 litres respectively). These particular standard English measures date from 1816, but their origins go back to the 10th century when King Edgar (reigned AD 959–975) decreed that standard weights be kept at Winchester and London. They were used to settle disputes, especially when they involved tithes. Winchester measures finally became redundant in 1824 when the Imperial system was introduced, though many Winchester equivalents remain in the United States. Further down the village, the 18th-century Bourton House has a 16th-century barn in its grounds.

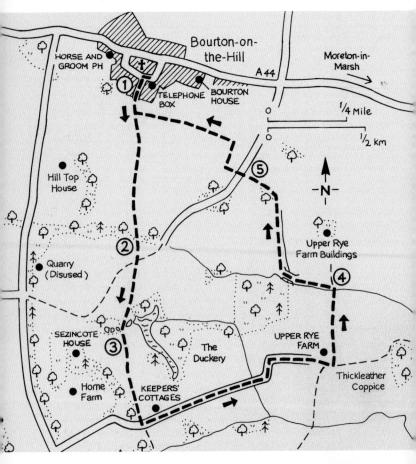

Walk 7 Directions

① Walk up the road from the **telephone box** with the church to your right. Turn left down a signposted track between walls. Go through a gate into a field and then continue forward to pass through two more gates.

> **WHILE YOU'RE THERE** ⓘ
> Both **Sezincote** and **Bourton House** are open to the public but have a limited season, so check their opening hours in advance. **Batsford Arboretum and Falconry** is only a mile (1.6km) away, just off the road to Moreton-in-Marsh.

② Cross a stile, followed by two kissing gates among the trees. This is the **Sezincote Estate** – go straight ahead, following markers and crossing a drive. Dip down to a gate among trees, with ponds on either side. Go ahead into a field, from where **Sezincote House** is visible to the right.

③ Walk into the next field and go right to the end, aiming for the top, right-hand corner. Pass through a gate to a narrow road and turn left. Walk down this road, passing the **keepers' cottages** to your left, and through a series of gates. The road

> **WHAT TO LOOK FOR** ⓘ
> As you start the walk look for a 'hole in the wall' just after the first gate. It consists of a tap located behind wooden doors just above ground, with the words '*Deo Gratias* AD 1919', inscribed in the wall above. I presume this is in gratitude for the end of the Great War. After Sezincote, as you walk down the road towards the farm, look for the buildings of the **Fire Service Technical College**, the main training centre for firefighters in the country.

will bottom out, curve left and right and then bring you to **Upper Rye Farm**. Pass to the right of the farmhouse, go through a gate and, immediately before a barn, turn left along a track and a road.

④ After a second cattle grid, go left over a stile. Follow the edge of the field to a footbridge. Go over it and turn right. Now follow the right-hand margin of the field to a stile in the far corner. Cross this to follow a path through woodland until you come to a stile and a field and continue on the same line to another stile.

> **WHERE TO EAT AND DRINK** ⓘ
> The **Horse and Groom** is a handsome old pub at the top of the village. Recently refurbished, it serves good lunches. In Moreton-in-Marsh seek out the **Marsh Goose**, a restaurant specialising in good quality local produce.

⑤ Cross a track to another stile and walk on. After a few paces, with Bourton-on-the-Hill plainly visible before you, turn right and follow the path to the next corner. Turn left and pass through three gates. After the third one, walk on for a few paces and turn right through a gate to return to the start.

Regenerating Bourton-on-the-Water

A walk on the wilder side of bustling Bourton-on-the-Water to see the results of its natural regeneration.

•DISTANCE•	4¾ miles (7.7km)
•MINIMUM TIME•	2hrs
•ASCENT / GRADIENT•	230ft (70m) ▲ ▲ ▲
•LEVEL OF DIFFICULTY•	쑈 쑈 쑈
•PATHS•	Track and field, can be muddy and wet in places, 26 stiles
•LANDSCAPE•	Sweeping valley views, lakes, streams, hills and village
•SUGGESTED MAP•	aqua3 OS Outdoor Leisure 45 The Cotswolds
•START / FINISH•	Grid reference: SP 169208
•DOG FRIENDLINESS•	Some stiles may be awkward for dogs; occasional livestock
•PARKING•	Pay-and-display car park on Station Road
•PUBLIC TOILETS•	At car park

BACKGROUND TO THE WALK

Despite Bourton-on-the-Water's popularity the throng is easily left behind by walking briefly eastwards to a chain of redundant gravel pits. In the 1970s these were landscaped and filled with water and fish. As is the way of these things, for some time the resulting lakes looked every inch the artificial creations they were, but now they have bedded into their surroundings and seem to be an integral part of the landscape.

Migrating Birds

The fish and water have acted as magnets for a range of wetland birds, whose populations rise and fall with the seasons. During the spring and summer months you should look out for the little grebe and the splendidly adorned great crested grebe, as well as the more familiar moorhens and coots, and mallard and tufted ducks. Wagtails will strut about the water's edge, swans and geese prowl across the water and kingfishers, if you are lucky, streak from bush to reed. Come the autumn, the number of birds will have increased significantly. Above all there will be vast numbers of ducks – pintail, shoveler, widgeon and pochard among them – as well as occasional visitors like cormorants. Either around the lakes or by the rivers you may also spy dippers and, in the hedgerows, members of the finch family.

Immigrant Birds

Should you get drawn into the village – as you surely will – keep listening for birdsong and you will hear some improbable 'visitors'. Bourton-on-the-Water has a large bird sanctuary which houses, among many other birds, one of the largest collections of penguins in the world, some of which featured in the film *Batman* (1989). A penguin seems an odd choice for an adversary, given its endearing reputation, and at first glance one might think that a penguin was a mammal and a bat was a bird, not vice versa. The reason for the presence of so many penguins in the Cotswolds is that the sanctuary's founder was also the owner of two small islands in the Falklands.

Long History

Penguins aside, Bourton-on-the-Water has a long history. The edge of the village is bounded by the Roman Fosse Way and many of its buildings are a pleasing mix of medieval, Georgian and Victorian. Although the village can become very crowded during the summer months, with the riverbanks at its centre like green beaches, strewn with people picnicking and paddling, it can still be charming. Arrive early enough in the morning, or hang around in the evening until the daytrippers have gone and you will find the series of bridges spanning the Windrush (one of which dates back to 1756) and the narrow streets beyond them highly picturesque. They retain the warm honeyed light that attracts people to the Cotswolds. You'll see far fewer visitors in little Clapton-on-the-Hill, which overlooks Bourton. Make the brief detour after Point ④ to see its handsome green and tiny church.

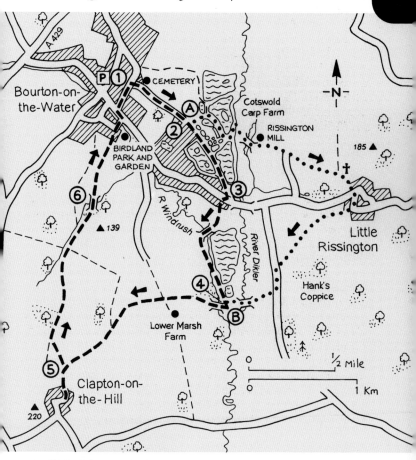

Walk 8 Directions

① Opposite the entrance to the main pay-and-display car park in **Bourton-on-the-Water** locate a public footpath and continue to a junction opposite the **cemetery**. Bear right to follow a lane all the way to its end. There are two gates in front of you (this is Point Ⓐ on Walk 9). Take the one on the right, with a stile beside it, to enter a grassy track.

Walk 8

② Follow the track between lakes to where it curves right. Leave the track to go forward over a bridge and stile into a field. Go across the field, curving right, to come to a stile at a road.

③ Cross the road, turn right and immediately left on to a track. After 100yds (91m) go left over a stile into a field and turn right. Cross a stile and return to the track, with a lake to your left. Just before a gate turn right over a bridge and left over a stile on to a path alongside the **River Windrush**. Continue until the path comes to a stile at a field. Turn left, cross another stile and go left over a bridge before turning right beside another lake.

> **WHAT TO LOOK FOR** ⓘ
> In the autumn, in particular, keep an eye out for **swans**. Mute swans – the most common type, with the orange bill – are present all the year round, but the whooper swan, with its erect neck and yellow bill, is only a winter visitor, flying in from northern Europe and Russia.

④ Where this second, smaller lake ends bear right to a stile (Point Ⓑ on Walk 9), followed by a bridge and stile at a field. Keep to the right side of fields until you come to a track. At a house leave the track and continue to a stile. In the next field, after 25yds (23m), turn left over a stile and then sharp right. Continue to a stile and then go half left across

> **WHERE TO EAT AND DRINK** ⓘ
> There are no pubs in Clapton. Bourton-on-the-Water has many pubs, tea shops and restaurants, catering to most tastes. Try the **Kingsbridge Inn** by the River Windrush, or the **Mousetrap** on Lansdown for reliable pub food. The **Old Manse**, also close to the river, serves a good lunch and dinner.

> **WHILE YOU'RE THERE** ⓘ
> Unlike other Cotswold villages, Bourton-on-the-Water has many and diverse attractions jostling for the contents of your wallet. The pick of these are probably **Birdland Park and Gardens** (► Background to the Walk) with their penguins, and the **Cotswold Motor Museum**, which has lots of pre-1950s cars as well as a few novelty items to thrill children. The most popular activity is arguably just strolling around.

a field. Continue on the same line across the next field to a stile. Cross this and follow the right margin of a field, to climb slowly to a junction of tracks. Turn left to visit the village of **Clapton-on-the-Hill**, or turn right to continue.

⑤ Follow a track to a field. Go forward then half right to pass right of **woodland**. Continue to a stile, followed by two stiles together at a field. Go half left to a stile and then follow a succession of stiles, a stream appearing to the left.

⑥ Cross a bridge and then go half right across a field to a bridge. Continue to more stiles and then walk along a grassy track towards houses. Cross one more stile and follow a path to a road in **Bourton**. Walk ahead to cross the river and turn left, then right, to return to the start.

Bourton, Clapton and Little Rissington

Extend Walk 8 with a diversion to Little Rissington.
See map and information panel for Walk 8

•DISTANCE•	6¾ miles (10.9km)
•MINIMUM TIME•	3hrs
•ASCENT / GRADIENT•	344ft (105m) ▲▲ ▲ ▲
•LEVEL OF DIFFICULTY•	林 林 林

Walk 9 Directions (Walk 8 option)

This walk takes you around further lakes, past a pretty mill and then up to Little Rissington, with its church that formerly served the nearby airfield – the original home to the Red Arrows display team.

At Point Ⓐ on Walk 8 bear left and, where the path forks, go right through a gate. After a few paces turn right along a narrow path, with a lake to your left. The path curves around the lake, coming to an end at a gate. Go through into a field and cross to a gate and stile. Cross the following meadow, bearing slightly to the right until you come to the banks of a stream.

Turn right, with the stream to your left, until you come to a stile and bridge on your left. Cross this and then another immediately after. With the wall of **Rissington Mill** close to your left, continue to a kissing gate. Pass into a field and continue on to a stile. Cross to a drive and walk straight along it. Where the drive curves right, cross a stile on your left into a field. Go

half right to a hedge, locate a bridge stile and cross into a field. Head up the field to the top, right-hand corner and a stile. Then walk straight across the next field to a point just left of the **church**.

Turn right into the churchyard, walk around the church and leave on the other side to follow a path to a road at the edge of **Little Rissington**. Cross the road (taking great care) and follow the lane opposite through the village. Where the lane goes sharp left, continue along a track and, after 20yds (18m), turn right down a track at the edge of a field.

After 250yds (229m), where the path opens up to a paddock, bear half left across it to a gate. Go through and continue down to a stile. Cross this, turn sharp left to another stile and, in the next field, go half right. Follow this same line down a succession of fields to arrive eventually at a lane.

Turn left for 100yds (91m) and then turn right along a path. This will take you over stiles and then a bridge before arriving at the head of a lake. Cross to the other side and then bear left to Point Ⓑ.

Fairford and the River Coln

Take this easy route from one of Gloucestershire's medieval wool towns to return by the river's edge.

•DISTANCE•	3¾ miles (6km)
•MINIMUM TIME•	1hr 30min
•ASCENT / GRADIENT•	15ft (5m)
•LEVEL OF DIFFICULTY•	
•PATHS•	Fields, tracks, riverside, can be muddy after rain, 6 stiles
•LANDSCAPE•	Water-meadows, river and village
•SUGGESTED MAP•	aqua3 OS Outdoor Leisure 45 The Cotswolds
•START / FINISH•	Grid reference: SP 152011
•DOG FRIENDLINESS•	Good but lots of swans and ducks along riverside
•PARKING•	On High Street near church
•PUBLIC TOILETS•	Near parking

Walk 10 Directions

This walk takes you out of town to the old gravel pits and back along the river. Walk up the **High Street**, with the church to your left (have a look at it at the end of the walk), and turn left into **Mill Lane**.

As the street name suggests, Fairford, like so many other small towns in the Cotswolds, owes its original importance to the medieval wool trade, and to one family in particular, the Tames. They were wool merchants and it was their money that embellished St Mary's Church, one of the great Cotswold wool churches. It was a family affair. The 16th-century writer and antiquary, John Leland, wrote, 'John Tame began the fair new chirche of Fairforde, and Edmund Tame finished it'. John Tame bought the manor and in fact rebuilt the church on the foundations of its predecessor, which had been built in Early English style.

Follow **Mill Lane** to the old mill and bridge. Then you come to a little garden flanked on two sides by an ancient shelter consisting of a stone slate roof supported by withered wooden pillars. About 150yds (137m) beyond this turn left over a stile into a meadow. Go straight across to the other side, pass through a gate and nip over a stile to a road.

Cross the road and enter **Waterloo Lane**, staying on this as it becomes a footpath. Where the football pitches come to an end, bear left along a footpath behind some houses. Stay on the path and then continue along the side of a

WHAT TO LOOK FOR ⓘ

As you pass the mill at the beginning of the walk look to the right and you will be looking into what is left of the estate of **Park House**, which was demolished in 1955. The most obvious reminder is the elegant bridge just beyond the mill pool. **Keble House**, on London Road, was the birthplace of the poet and theologian, John Keble.

> **WHILE YOU'RE THERE** ⓘ
>
> It's difficult to avoid the presence of the military, particularly NATO's air forces in the Cotswolds. So why not make the most of it and take in the RAF Benevolent Fund's annual **international air tattoo**, usually in July at RAF Fairford, to the south of the town.

meadow. Follow a track to the right of a cottage to a junction.

Turn left to enter a farmyard and then turn right, aiming for a point to the right of another cottage. Pass the cottage and cross a stile into a field. Bear left to stay right of the river, to meet a stile at the edge of **woodland**. Cross on to a wide grassy track and walk along here to the left of woodland, the river on your left. Where the woods come to an end and the field opens up, bear half left to pass beneath the electricity cables and find a stile and bridge in the far corner, amongst bushes and trees.

Cross these, enter woodland and follow the footpath to a bridge across the river. On the other side, enter an area of **lakes** – former gravel pits. Walk anti-clockwise around the first lake and on the other side, 150yds (137m) after passing two protruding hedges, look for a path on the right between trees. Where this comes to an end turn left along a track. Keep going until you come to a bridge on your right. Cross this and then join the bank of the river.

Whilst Fairford lies on the banks of the River Coln, where it meanders peacefully across a flat landscape of meadows and woodland, the town has an association with noise. Concorde was tested at the nearby airbase and, over the last few

decades, it has served as a base for various military campaigns around the world. Every year there is a huge air tattoo here, in aid of the RAF's Benevolent Fund. Follow the riverbank all the way to a bridge over the river. Turn right here.

St Mary's Church in Fairford was built in late Perpendicular style. It is a striking building but its most famous feature is the near-complete set of medieval stained windows, perhaps unique in the country. They were made in the late 15th century (a few years before John Tame's death in 1500), probably by the Flemish craftsman, Barnard Flower, with the help of English and French artisans. Flower was also employed by Henry VIII to carry out work at Westminster Abbey and at King's College in Cambridge.

Follow the path you are on and it will lead you back into **Fairford**, to visit the church prior to returning to your car. The idea of the windows in St Mary's is to explain the Christian faith as if the onlooker were turning the pages of a picture book. They are arranged symmetrically. For example, on one wall are windows depicting twelve prophets, opposite which are depicted the twelve apostles. The journey around the church, bathed in the magical light thrown down by the windows, is a memorable one. There are other things to admire here: John Tame's tomb, the amusing misericord seats in the chancel and the gravestone of Tiddles the cat in the churchyard.

> **WHERE TO EAT AND DRINK** ⓘ
>
> There is a choice of several pubs and cafes in Fairford. The **Bull**, on the High Street near the church, is a nice old pub and convenient for this walk.

Blockley, Batsford and the Arboretum

The exotic legacy of a 19th-century diplomat adorns this part of the Cotswold escarpment.

•DISTANCE•	4½ miles (7.2km)
•MINIMUM TIME•	2hrs
•ASCENT / GRADIENT•	410ft (125m) ▲▲ ▲
•LEVEL OF DIFFICULTY•	秫 秫 秫
•PATHS•	Lanes, tracks and fields, 8 stiles
•LANDSCAPE•	Woodland, hills with good views and villages
•SUGGESTED MAP•	aqua3 OS Outdoor Leisure 45 The Cotswolds
•START / FINISH•	Grid reference: SP 165348
•DOG FRIENDLINESS•	Some good lengthy stretches without livestock
•PARKING•	On B4479 below Blockley church
•PUBLIC TOILETS•	On edge of churchyard, just off main street in Blockley

BACKGROUND TO THE WALK

England seems to be a country of trees – it is a feature that visitors often remark on. Walking through Gloucestershire you are surrounded by many native species but, when you visit Batsford Arboretum, you will encounter 50 acres (20.3ha) of woodland containing over 1,000 species of trees and shrubs from all over the world, particularly from China, Japan and North America.

The Japanese Connection

The arboretum was originally a garden created in the 1880s by the traveller and diplomat, Bertie Mitford, 1st Lord Redesdale, grandfather to the renowned Mitford sisters. Posted as an attaché to the British Embassy in Tokyo, he became deeply influenced by the Far East. Throughout the park there are bronze statues, brought from Japan by Bertie Mitford, and a wide range of bamboos. After the 1st Lord Dulverton purchased Batsford in 1920, his son transformed the garden into the arboretum we see today, with its 90 species of magnolia, maples, cherry trees and conifers, all in a beautiful setting on the Cotswold escarpment. Batsford village is comparatively recent, having grown up at the gates of Batsford Park, a neo-Tudor house built between 1888 and 1892 by Ernest George. He built it for Lord Redesdale to replace an earlier, Georgian house. (It is not open to the public but is clearly visible from the arboretum.) Batsford church was constructed a little before the house, in 1862, in a neo-Norman style. It has several monuments to the Mitford family and a fine work by the sculptor Joseph Nollekens from 1808.

Silky Blockley

This walk starts in the unspoilt village of Blockley. It was originally owned by the bishops of Worcester but it didn't really begin to prosper until the 19th century. At one time no fewer than six silk mills, employing over 500 employees, were driven by Blockley's fast-flowing stream. Their silks went mostly to Coventry for the production of ribbon. Blockley's history is both enlightened and superstitious. It was one of the first villages in the world to have electric light: in the 1880s Dovedale House was illuminated through Lord Edward Spencer-Churchill's use of water to run a dynamo. In the early part of that same century the millenarian prophetess, Joanna Southcott, lived in the village until her death in 1814. The tower of Blockley's substantial church predates the silk boom by only 100 years or so, but inside the church are several imposing monuments to the owners of the local mansion, Northwick Park. At least two of these are by the eminent 18th-century sculptor, John Michael Rysbrack (1694–1770). The village itself has an air of unassuming beauty, its main street lined with a mixture of houses and cottages from the 17th, 18th, and 19th centuries.

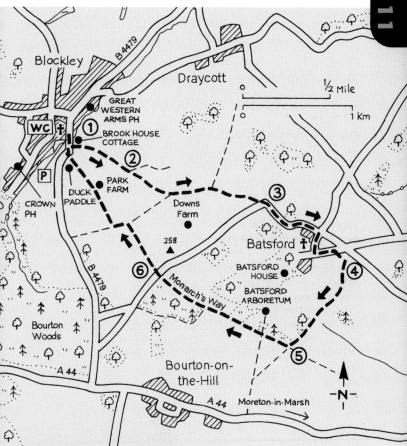

Walk 11 Directions

① Walk along the road with the church above you to your right. Continue ahead, pass **Brook House Cottage**, then turn left immediately, up a lane. Follow this as it ascends for ¼ mile (400m) until it bears left.

② Continue ahead to pass to the right-hand side of a barn. Pass through a gate and in the next field follow its right-hand boundary to another gate. Pass through this to stay on the left side of the next field. Pass into yet another field and then go half right to a gate leading out to a road.

Walk 11

> **WHILE YOU'RE THERE**   ⓘ
>
> A short distance to the west of Blockley is **Upton**, the site of a medieval village that disappeared. Although recorded in the Domesday Book, it is likely that Upton's inhabitants were forced out by the bishops of Worcester who sequestered the land for use as sheep pastures. Whilst there isn't a great deal to see on the ground, this is one of the few abandoned villages to have been excavated by archaeologists.

③ Turn left and follow the road down to a crossroads. Turn right to pass through **Batsford** village to a junction (from where you can visit the church on the right). Bear left, and, at the next junction, turn right.

④ After a few paces turn right on to a footpath and follow this through a succession of fields, negotiating stiles and gates where they arise. **Batsford House** will be visible above you to the right.

> **WHERE TO EAT AND DRINK**   ⓘ
>
> Blockley is one of those rare creatures in the Cotswolds, a village with both a pub and a shop. The pub, the **Crown**, is also a hotel and it serves excellent lunches of all descriptions. There is also the **Great Western Arms**, on Station Road, named after the railway service, which in fact came no closer than Paxford.

⑤ Finally, go through a gate into a ribbed field and turn right to a stile just left of a house at a drive. Cross this (the entrance to **Batsford Arboretum**), pass through a gate and follow the path up the field to a stile. Cross and continue to a track. Follow this up until where it bears left. Turn right on to a path and almost immediately left at a wall, to continue the ascent. Keep going until you reach a road.

⑥ Cross the road to go through a gate and pass through two fields until you come to a path among trees. Turn left, go through another gate, and, after a few paces, turn right over a stile into a field with **Blockley** below you. Continue down to a stile at the bottom. Cross into the next field and pass beneath **Park Farm** on your right. Bear gently left, crossing stiles, along the **Duck Paddle**, until you come to a road. Turn right and return to your starting point in the village.

> **WHAT TO LOOK FOR**   ⓘ
>
> An unusual feature of Blockley is its **raised footpaths**, running along the main street. It was noted in the 19th century that 'many dangerous accidents were occurring'. A parish waywarden of the day, Richard Belcher, added iron posts and railings, 'setting the unemployed to work in January and February'. At the south western end of the High Street is **Rock Cottage** where the prophetess, Joanna Southcott, lived.

Gloucestershire's Gardens Around Mickleton

A walk that takes you past Kiftsgate Court and Hidcote Manor Garden, two early 20th-century creations of international repute.

•DISTANCE•	5½ miles (8.8km)
•MINIMUM TIME•	2hrs 30min
•ASCENT / GRADIENT•	625ft (190m) ▲▲▲
•LEVEL OF DIFFICULTY•	🚶 🚶 🚶
•PATHS•	Fields, firm tracks, some possibly muddy woodland, 12 stiles
•LANDSCAPE•	Woodland, open hills and villages
•SUGGESTED MAP•	aqua3 OS Explorer 205 Stratford-upon-Avon & Evesham
•START / FINISH•	Grid reference: SP 162434
•DOG FRIENDLINESS•	On leads in livestock fields, good open stretches elsewhere
•PARKING•	Free car park at church
•PUBLIC TOILETS•	None on route

BACKGROUND TO THE WALK

This walk takes you within striking distance of two of the finest planned gardens in the country. The first, Kiftsgate Court, is the lesser known of the two but nonetheless demands a visit. The house itself is primarily Victorian, whilst the garden was created immediately after World War One by Heather Muir, who was a close friend of Major Johnston, the creator of the nearby Hidcote Manor Garden. Kiftsgate's gardens are designed around a steep hillside overlooking the village of Mickleton and the Vale of Evesham, with terraces, paths, flowerbeds and shrubs. The layout is in the form of rooms and the emphasis appears to be more on the plants themselves, rather than on the overall design. The steeper part of the garden is almost a cliff. It's clad in pine trees and boasts wonderful views across the vale below.

Major Johnson's Rooms

The second horticultural treat is Hidcote Manor Garden, part of the little hamlet of Hidcote Bartrim. This garden is the fruit of over 40 years of work by Major Lawrence Johnson, an East Coast American who purchased the 17th-century manor house in 1907 and gave it to the National Trust in 1948. Many people consider it be one of the greatest of English gardens, and certainly it is one of the most influential. Hidcote grew from almost nothing – when Major Johnson first arrived there was a just a cedar tree and a handful of beeches on 11 acres (4.5ha) of open wold. To some extent it reconciles the formal and informal schools of garden design. Hidcote is not one garden but several. Like Kiftsgate it is laid out in a series of 'outdoor rooms', as they have been described, with walls of stone and of hornbeam, yew and box hedge. These rooms are themed, having names such the White Garden and the Fuchsia Garden, for example. There is also a wild garden growing around a stream, as well as lawns and carefully placed garden ornaments that help to create a bridge between the order within and the disorder without.

Have a Butchers

This walk begins in Mickleton, at the foot of the Cotswold escarpment, below these two fine gardens. Clearly a Cotswold village, notwithstanding its mixture of stone, thatch and timber, the parish church at the village edge, lurks behind a striking house in the so-called Cotswold Queen Anne style. It has a 14th-century tower and an interesting monument to the 18th-century quarry owner from Chipping Campden, Thomas Woodward. Near the hotel in the village centre is a Victorian memorial fountain designed by William Burges, the architect behind Cardiff Castle. There is also a fine butcher's shop here, a sight to behold, especially in autumn, when it's festooned with locally shot pheasant. As if to further enhance the village's Cotwold credentials, this was also the birthplace of Endymion Porter, a patron of the Cotswold Olimpick Games on Dover's Hill (▶ Walk 13).

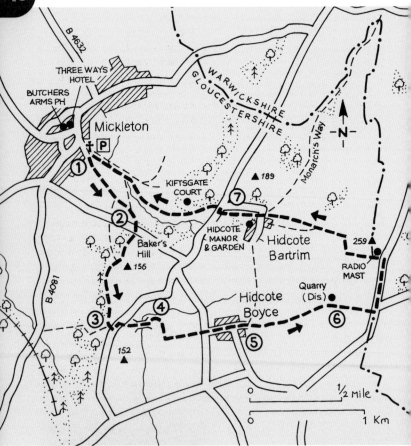

Walk 12 **Directions**

① With the **church** to your left, turn right up a bank to a gate. Cross a field on a left diagonal to a gate at a thicket. Follow a path through the trees. Emerge into a field and follow its left margin to a gate at the end.

② In the next field go half right to a gate in the corner. Cross a road and go up some steps to a stile. Turn right to walk around the edge

WHILE YOU'RE THERE

It would be a shame to miss the two fine gardens. **Kiftsgate Court** is open 2–6 on Wednesday, Thursday, Sunday and public holidays during April, May, August and September. In June and July it is open 12–6 on Wednesday, Thursday, Saturday and Sunday. Homemade teas are available but dogs are not welcome. Just up the road, **Hidcote Manor Garden** is owned by the National Trust and is open daily, 10:30–6:30. Closed Thursday and Friday, March–November, except June and July, when it's closed Friday only. It can get crowded, but there is a good resaurant and plant sales centre.

of the field as it bears left. After 250yds (229m), take a path among trees, a steep bank eventually appearing down to the right. The path brings you to a field and then to a barn.

③ At the barn turn left on to a track. Just about opposite, keep left of a hedge, following the edge of a field to the bottom corner. Go through a gap to a bridge across a stream and turn left.

WHAT TO LOOK FOR

In **Hidcote Boyce** some of the houses, though built of stone broadly in the Cotswold style, are unusually tall. There doesn't seem to be any good reason for this, but the style is almost unique to the village. Climbing the hill out of Hidcote Bartrim, you will find yourself in an area of bumps and hillocks – these are the remains of an old stone quarry.

④ Follow the margin of the field as it goes right and then right again. Continue until you come to a gate on the left. Go through this and walk until you reach another gate at a road. Walk ahead through **Hidcote Boyce**. Where the road goes right, stay ahead to pass through a farmyard.

⑤ Beyond a gate take a rising track for just over ¼ mile (400m). Where this track appears to fork, stay to the left to enter a field. Bear left and then right around a hedge and head for a gate. In an area of grassy

mounds stay to the left of a barn and head for a gate visible in the top left corner.

⑥ Follow the next field edge to a road. Turn sharp left to follow the lesser road. Immediately before a radio transmission mast turn left on to a track and follow this all the way down to pass to the right of **Hidcote Manor Garden**. After passing the garden's main entrance go left through a gate into shrubland and turn right. Follow the path to a field and cross it to a gate on the far side.

⑦ At the road turn right and then, before **Kiftsgate Court**, turn left through a gate and descend through a field. Pass through some trees and follow the left-hand side of the next field until you come to a gate on the left. Go through this and cross to another gate. Follow the edge of the next field. Where the field opens up head just to the left of **Mickleton church**. Go through a gate leading between the two cemeteries to return to the start.

WHERE TO EAT AND DRINK

In Mickleton the **Butcher's Arms** serves good pub food, and the **Three Ways Hotel** is recommended for its puddings in particular. It's the home of the famous 'Pudding Club', where you can taste the finest in traditional English desserts. There is also a restaurant at **Hidcote Manor Garden** and a tea room at Kiftsgate Court

Olimpick Playground Near Chipping Campden

Walk out from the Cotswolds' most beautiful wool town to Dover's Hill, the spectacular site of centuries-old Whitsuntide festivities.

•DISTANCE•	5 miles (8km)
•MINIMUM TIME•	2hrs
•ASCENT / GRADIENT•	280ft (85m) ▲▲ ▲▲
•LEVEL OF DIFFICULTY•	术术 术术 术术
•PATHS•	Fields, roads and tracks, 8 stiles
•LANDSCAPE•	Open hillside, woodland and village
•SUGGESTED MAP•	aqua3 OS Outdoor Leisure 45 The Cotswolds
•START / FINISH•	Grid reference: SP 151391
•DOG FRIENDLINESS•	Suitable in parts (Dover's Hill) but livestock in some fields
•PARKING•	Chipping Campden High Street or main square
•PUBLIC TOILETS•	A short way down Sheep Street

BACKGROUND TO THE WALK

The Cotswold Olimpicks bear only a passing resemblance to their more famous international counterpart. What they lack in grandeur and razzmatazz, however, they make up for in picturesqueness and local passion. Far from being a multi-million dollar shrine to technology, the stadium is a natural amphitheatre – the summit of Dover's Hill, on the edge of the Cotswold escarpment. The hill, with spectacular views westwards over the Vale of Evesham, is an English version of the site of the Greek original.

Royal Assent

Dover's Hill is named after the founder of the Cotswold Olimpicks, Robert Dover. Established with the permission of James I, they were dubbed 'royal' games, and indeed have taken place during the reign of 14 monarchs. Dover was born in Norfolk in 1582. He was educated at Cambridge and then was called to the bar. His profession brought him to the Cotswolds but he had memories of the plays and spectacles that he had seen in the capital, for this was the era of Shakespeare. It is generally accepted that the first games took place in 1612, but they may well have begun at an earlier date. It is also possible that Dover was simply reviving an existing ancient festivity. Initially, at least, the main events were horse-racing and hare-coursing, the prizes being, respectively, a silver castle ornament and a silver-studded collar. Other competitions in these early games were for running, jumping, throwing, wrestling and staff fighting. The area was festooned with yellow flags and ribbons and there were many dancing events as well as pavilions for chess and other similarly cerebral contests.

Annual Event

The Olimpicks soon became an indispensable part of the local Whitsuntide festivities, with mention of them even being made in Shakespeare's work. Dover managed the games for 30 years and he died in 1652. The games continued in various forms throughout the following centuries, surviving attempts to suppress them when they became more rowdy, and finally becoming an established annual event once again in 1966. Nowadays, the games are a cross between pantomime and carnival but have somehow retained their atmosphere of local showmanship. At the end of the evening all the spectators, holding flaming torches, file down the road back to Chipping Campden, where the festivities continue with dancing and music along the main street and in the square.

The Wool Town

It's worth lingering in Chipping Campden, before or after the walk. Possibly the most beautiful of all the Cotswold towns, it was once famous throughout Europe as the centre of the English wool trade. A leisurely stroll along its curving High Street of handsome stone houses should be an essential part of your visit. The church too is particularly fine and it's also worthwhile searching out the Ernest Wilson Memorial Garden, on the High Street.

Walk 13

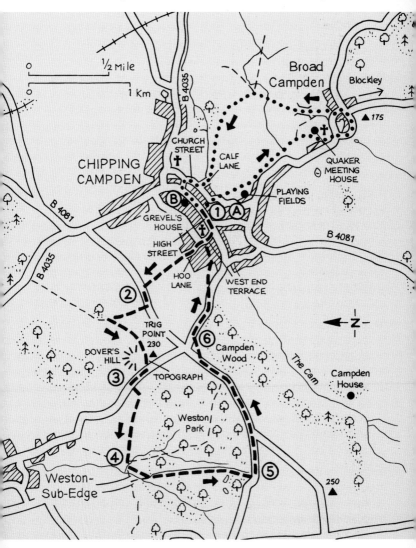

Walk 13 **Directions**

① Turn left from the **Noel Arms** (Point Ⓐ on Walk 14), continue to the **Catholic church**, and turn right into **West End Terrace**. Where this bears right, go straight ahead on **Hoo Lane**. Follow this up to a right turn, with farm buildings on your left. Continue uphill over a stile to a path and keep going to a road.

② Turn left for a few paces and then right to cross to a path. Follow this along the field edge to a stile. Go over to **Dover's Hill** and follow the hedge to a stile with extensive views before you. Turn left along the escarpment edge, which drops away to your right. Pass a **trig point** and then a **topograph**. Now go right, down the slope, to a kissing gate on the left. Go through to a road and turn right.

WHILE YOU'RE THERE

Broadway Tower, with its associations with William Morris, stands about 4 miles (6.4km) to the south west of Chipping Campden. A Gothic folly, built in Portland stone in 1799, it glowers across the Vale of Evesham. There is an interesting small museum inside and fine views across the vale from the top.

③ After 150yds (137m) turn left over a stile into a field. Cross this and find a gate in the bottom right-hand corner. Head straight down the next field. At a stile go into another field and, keeping to the left of a fence, continue to another stile. Head down the next field, cross a track and then find adjacent stiles in the bottom left corner.

④ Cross the first one and walk along the bottom of a field. Keep the stream and fence to your right

and look for a stile in the far corner. Go over, crossing the stream, and then turn left, following a rising woodland path alongside the stream. Enter a field through a gate and continue ahead to meet a track. Stay on this, passing through gateposts, until you come to a country lane and turn left.

WHERE TO EAT AND DRINK

Chipping Campden has plenty of pubs, tea rooms and restaurants of all descriptions. **Badgers Hall**, on the High Street, does an exceptionally fine tea, whilst the **Seven Bells**, on Church Street, is a very relaxing pub.

⑤ After 400yds (366m) reach a busier road and turn left for a further 450yds (411m). Shortly before the road curves left, drop to the right on to a field path parallel with the road. About 200yds (183m) before the next corner go half right down the field to a road.

⑥ Turn right, down the road. Shortly after a cottage on the right, go left into a field. Turn right over a stile and go half left to the corner. Pass through a kissing gate, cross a road among houses and continue ahead to meet **West End Terrace**. Turn right to return to the centre of **Chipping Campden**.

WHAT TO LOOK FOR

On reaching Dover's Hill, the route almost doubles back on itself –this is necessary in order to observe legal rights of way. Spend a little time poring over the **topograph** – on a clear day there is much to try to identify. In Campden, look out for the 14th-century **Grevel's House**, opposite Church Lane. William Grevel, called 'the flower of the wool merchants of all England', is thought to have been the inspiration for the merchant in *The Canterbury Tales*.

The Broad Way

Extend Walk 13 with a short diversion to nearby Broad Campden.
See map and information panel for Walk 13

•DISTANCE•	2¾ miles (4.4km)
•MINIMUM TIME•	1 hr 15 min
•ASCENT / GRADIENT•	180ft (55m) ▲ ▲ ▲
•LEVEL OF DIFFICULTY•	秋 秋 秋

Walk 14 Directions (Walk 13 option)

Chipping Campden's near neighbour, Broad Campden, does not have a spectacular high street, nor even much of a church. It does have some exceptionally pretty houses (several of which, unusually for the Cotswolds, are thatched), an attractive pub and a 17th-century Quaker's Meeting House, all in a snug, overlooked fold of the Cotswold countryside.

From the **High Street**, walk through the arch next to the **Noel Arms Hotel** (Point Ⓐ) and continue ahead to join a path. Pass playing fields to reach a junction with a road. Go left here, into a field, then immediately right, to follow the field edge parallel with the road. After 600yds (549m) fork right to a gate. Enter a drive, walk past a house and then leave the drive to walk ahead to a gate. Pass through into an alley and follow it to pass the **Quaker's Meeting House**.

Emerge at the green with the church to your left. At a junction continue ahead to walk through the village. The road bears left and straightens. After the turning for Blockley, go left down a road marked 'Unsuitable for Motors'. After 70yds (64m) turn right along the drive of '**Hollybush**'. Pass through a gate and then another to continue along the left, lower margin of an **orchard**.

Cross a stile, then a bridge and turn sharp right along the right-hand field edge, with the stream on your right. Cross the stream at the end of the field and, in the next field, go straight across, bearing right to a gap. Go up the next field to a stile and cross into a field. Turn left and then go half right to pass to the right of a house.

Cross a stile, then go half right to a gate. Go through and bear right, down to another stile in the corner. In the next field go half right, with **Chipping Campden church** away to the right, to approach a stream near a stone arch. Do not cross the stream but, 70yds (64m) after the arch, turn right through a gate and follow the path as it turns left to a drive. Turn right and follow the drive to **Calf Lane**. Turn right and, at the top, turn left into **Church Street** (Point Ⓑ) to return to a junction with the main street (or right to visit the magnificent church). Turn left to return to the start of the walk.

Walk 15

Roman Ways at Condicote

Following the course of Ryknild Street across the high wolds.

•DISTANCE•	8¾ miles (14.1km)
•MINIMUM TIME•	3hrs 15min
•ASCENT / GRADIENT•	263ft (80m) ▲ ▲ ▲
•LEVEL OF DIFFICULTY•	🚶 🚶 🚶
•PATHS•	Track, field, estate road and country lanes, 8 stiles
•LANDSCAPE•	Long views across high wolds, estate land, villages
•SUGGESTED MAP•	aqua3 OS Outdoor Leisure 45, The Cotswolds
•START / FINISH•	Grid reference: SP 151282
•DOG FRIENDLINESS•	Nice long stretches of track. Some livestock in parts
•PARKING•	Condicote village
•PUBLIC TOILETS•	None on route

Walk 15 Directions

During the first portion of this walk, you will be following the unmistakable line of a Roman Road, Ryknild Street, which extended from the Fosse Way near Bourton-on-the-Water in a north westerly direction, crossed Watling Street near Lichfield and turned north east to terminate at Templeborough, near Rotherham. The stretch you will be walking along may not, you can imagine, have changed much in 2,000 years, even if the ordered landscape that rolls away on either side would not, perhaps, be immediately recognisable to travellers of the era.

It is well known that the Romans built remarkably straight roads throughout Britannia, with a total length of about 10,000 miles (16,000km), most of which was built during the first 100 years of occupation – a mile (1.6km) of road every four days. Later roads were not as well built as the earlier ones – road building has always

been an expensive business and the Romans sometimes found it expedient not to insist on straight lines. Nonetheless, the overall level of skill involved was extraordinarily high, with roads built on the same line over vast distances.

Roads were not a brand new phenomenon, as various 'ways', usually on high ground, following ridges, had been existence for centuries before the Romans arrived. What was new was the quality of the road building and the comprehensiveness of the road network. The basic aim was to link sites with water supplies, which were located a day's march apart (10–15 miles/16–24km). Alignments were laid out from hilltop to hilltop and then with intermediate points between. Some

---

WHERE TO EAT AND DRINK ⓘ

The only place on the route is the **Lords of the Manor Hotel** in Upper Slaughter. This is a luxurious hotel with an excellent restaurant (prepare to remove your boots). Otherwise, head into Stow-on-the-Wold, only 4 miles (6.4km) away.

zig-zagging was permitted but only for good reasons – hill cuttings, for example, were rarely used, perhaps only as early military roads. Marshes were not considered an obstacle and roads were built across them by the copious use of brushwood. Fording was preferred to bridges presumably for reasons of cost and longevity. What bridges there were would, in any case, have been built of wood and have therefore long since disappeared.

> **WHILE YOU'RE THERE**
> South east of Condicote is Donnington and, not far from it, the **Donnington Brewery**. This small, independent concern is not open to the public but located alongside a small lake it must be one of the most picturesque breweries in the country. You can taste their excellent brews at the **Fox** in nearby Broadwell.

> **WHAT TO LOOK FOR**
> Half way through the walk you will pass through the domain of **Eyeford Park**. You may be able to catch glimpses of this elegant house, built in 1910 in Queen Anne style by Sir Guy Dawber on the site of an earlier mansion where William III was once the guest of Charles Talbot, Duke of Shrewsbury.

The procedure for the construction of the road itself might consist initially of woodland clearance to the tune of a 90ft (27.4m) line, marked by ploughed outer ditches, followed by two more drainage ditches about 30ft (9m) apart that provided the outer limits of the road itself. Material from around about would be dug up and used to build up the roadway. On top of this would go local stone, followed by rubble, or gravel, which would then be cambered. Most of Ryknild Street may seem like a very straight farm track but its solid foundations are 2,000 years old.

From **Condicote village green**, take the road south out of the village, near the stone cross. Follow it to a junction and go straight ahead on to a track, the remains of **Ryknild Street**. As you might expect, the route is clear – follow this track for just under 2 miles (3.2km), crossing roads with care where they arise. The section after the **B4068** is a surfaced road which will bring you to a T-junction. Cross to a gate and then a field to a stile. In the next field, curve right to a stile at the edge of woodland. Cross an estate road to follow a woodland path to a gate at the edge of a field. Curve left to follow a fence down the field to a gate in the corner. Turn right along the road. After 100yds (91m) go left over a stile and turn immediately right. Go through a succession of fields, finally dipping down to a gate and a bridge over a stream. Follow a path up to **Upper Slaughter** and turn left. At the village square turn right and head towards the river. After the last cottage on the left, turn left, with the river to the right, to follow a path past a house and then among trees. Follow this into grassland and up to gates beside a cottage. Descend through trees to a road. Turn left and walk along the road for about 250yds (229m), using the verge where possible. Just before cottages turn right on to a metalled drive rising up through trees. This will take you past **Eyford Park**. Stay on this in its various forms as track and drive all the way to a road. At the road, turn right for ¾ mile (1.2km) and at a junction turn left. Follow this to another road. Cross over and continue until you come to the road on your left leading back into Condicote.

Musing on the Past at Northleach

A modest Cotswold village is home to a pair of diverse museums.

•DISTANCE•	4 miles (6.4km)
•MINIMUM TIME•	1hr 45min
•ASCENT / GRADIENT•	165ft (50m) ▲▲ ▲ ▲
•LEVEL OF DIFFICULTY•	🚶 🚶🚶 🚶🚶
•PATHS•	Fields, tracks and pavement, one stretch muddy after rain, 3 stiles
•LANDSCAPE•	Valley track, wolds and villages
•SUGGESTED MAP•	aqua3 OS Outdoor Leisure 45 The Cotswolds
•START / FINISH•	Grid reference: SP 113145
•DOG FRIENDLINESS•	Some clear stretches without livestock, few stiles
•PARKING•	Northleach village square
•PUBLIC TOILETS•	In village square

BACKGROUND TO THE WALK

For a small country village to have one museum is unusual – to have two, as Northleach does, is remarkable. One, the Cotswold Countryside Collection, is closely associated with its surroundings; the other, Keith Harding's World of Mechanical Music, is one of those eccentricities that has, by happenstance, ended up here in Northleach.

Mechanical Music Museum

The World of Mechanical Music is in the High Street at Oak House, a former wool house, pub and school. There are daily demonstrations of all manner of mechanical musical instruments, as well as musical boxes, clocks and automata. Some of the instruments, early examples of 'canned' music, date back more than 200 years. The presentation is simultaneously erudite and light-hearted. (You may also listen to early, live recordings of concerts given by some of the great composers including Gershwin and Grieg.) This is something more than a museum – both serious historical research and highly accomplished repairs are carried out here.

House of Correction

To the west of the village centre, at a corner of a Fosse Way crossroads, lies the Cotswold Countryside Collection. It is housed in an 18th-century prison, or 'house of correction', built by a prison reformer and wealthy philanthropist, Sir Onesipherous Paul. He was a descendant of a family of successful clothiers from Woodchester, near Stroud, who were also responsible for the construction of, what is now, the Prince of Wales's house at Highgrove. Paul's intentions were surely good, but conditions in the prison were still harsh and the treadmill was still considered effective as the unrelenting instrument of slow punishment. As well as a restored 18th-century cell block, you'll find the museum houses an interesting collection of agricultural implements and machinery, and displays plenty of fascinating photographs showing what rural life in the Cotswolds was once like.

Walk 16

Then and Now

Northleach itself, like Cirencester and Chipping Campden, was one of the key medieval wool trading centres of the Cotswolds and therefore also one of the most important towns in Europe. Though once on a crossroads of the A40 and the Fosse Way, neither now passes through the town, the completion of the A40 bypass in the mid-1980s leaving the town centre a quiet and very attractive place to visit.

The main street is lined with houses, some half-timbered, dating from between the 16th and 19th centuries. Many of these retain their ancient 'burgage' plots at the rear that would originally have served as market gardens. Above the market square is a tiny maze of narrow lanes, overlooked by the Church of St Peter and St Paul, the town's impressive 15th-century Perpendicular 'wool church'. Its features include an array of brasses commemorating the wool merchants on whose wealth the church and town were founded.

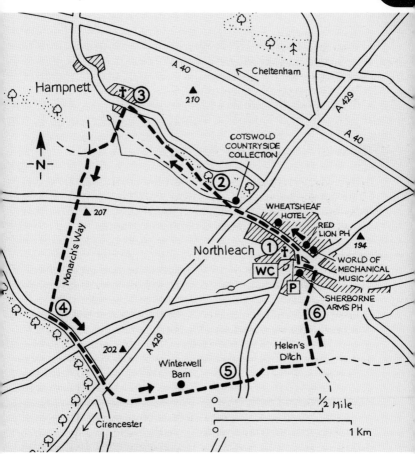

Walk 16 Directions

① From **Northleach square**, with the church behind you, turn left and walk along the main street to the traffic lights at the **A429**. Cross with care, keep left of the **Cotswold Countryside Collection** and, immediately after passing the museum, turn right through a gate into a field. Go ahead, turn left with the river to your right and then turn right to cross the river into the next field.

② Turn left and go half right up the field to a stile. Go over this into the next field and, keeping fairly close to the field's right-hand margin, head for another stile on the far side. Pass into the next field and follow a path across it in the general direction of **Hampnett church**. This will bring you to a gate at a road.

> **WHAT TO LOOK FOR** ⓘ
> Leaving Northleach, look out for some interesting old houses. **Walton House**, for example, was formerly the King's Head, an important inn on the old London to Gloucester route. Further on, set back from the road, are the buildings of the old brewery.

③ Turn left and almost immediately come to a track on your left. To visit the church walk ahead and then return to this track. Otherwise, turn left down the track and follow it as it descends to pass farm buildings. Where the track begins to bear right, turn left to climb a track towards a gate. Go through it and continue to follow the track, eventually striking a road. Cross this to walk along another track all the way to another road.

④ At this road turn left and walk until you reach the **A429**. Cross with great care to a gate and then walk along a track until you come

> **WHERE TO EAT AND DRINK** ⓘ
> Although only fairly small Northleach has two pubs, the **Red Lion** and the **Sherborne Arms**, and a hotel, the **Wheatsheaf**. Further along the Fosse Way is the **Fossebridge Inn**, located in a hollow in a rare curve in the Fosse Way, with a large garden beside a stream.

to a farmyard. Walk through the yard and out the other side along a track to another road.

⑤ Cross to a track and follow this for 500yds (457m). Turn left through a gap in a hedge to enter a field and follow the left margin with a stone wall to your left. **Northleach** will soon come into view. Where the field comes to an end, cross a stile and continue ahead, bearing slightly right, to a gate at the bottom of the next field, beside a playground.

⑥ Go through and walk towards some tennis courts. Just before these, turn right to cross a stream. Walk the length of an alley and, at the top, turn left to return to the starting point.

> **WHILE YOU'RE THERE** ⓘ
> As well as the two fine **museums** in Northleach (► Background to the Walk), you are close to the National Trust's 4,000 acre (1,620ha) **Sherbourne Park Estate** (► Walk 4). This was bequeathed by Lord Sherborne in 1982 and includes the estate village and richly planted parkland. The highlight is Lodge Park, a17th-century deer course with an ornate grandstand boasting spectacular views. The grandstand has been extensively restored and can be visited only by prior arrangment. Call 01451 844794 for information.

Guiting Power to the People

A gentle ramble in quintessential Gloucestershire, from a typical village with an atypical place name and atypical ownership.

•DISTANCE•	5 miles (8km)
•MINIMUM TIME•	2hrs
•ASCENT / GRADIENT•	295ft (90m) ▲▲ ▲ ▲
•LEVEL OF DIFFICULTY•	🚶 🚶 🚶
•PATHS•	Fields, tracks and country lanes, 10 stiles
•LANDSCAPE•	Woodland, hills and village
•SUGGESTED MAP•	aqua3 OS Outdoor Leisure 45 The Cotswolds
•START / FINISH•	Grid reference: SP 094245
•DOG FRIENDLINESS•	Fairly clear of livestock but many horses on roads
•PARKING•	Car park outside village hall (small fee)
•PUBLIC TOILETS•	None on route

BACKGROUND TO THE WALK

It is remarkable how much detailed history is available about English villages, even ones, like Guiting Power, that are distinguished only by their comeliness. Looking from the village green, surrounded by stone cottages, with its church and secluded manor house, it is easy to imagine that very little has changed here in 1,000 years.

What's in a Name?

The eccentric name comes from the Saxon word 'gyte-ing', or torrent, and indeed the name was given not only to Guiting Power but also to neighbouring Temple Guiting, which in the 12th century was owned by the Knights Templars. Guiting Power though, was named after the pre-eminent local family of the 13th century, the Le Poers.

Over the years the village was variously known as Gything, Getinge, Gettinges Poer, Guyting Poher, Nether Guiting and Lower Guiting. Its current name and spelling date only from 1937. In 1086, the Domesday Book noted that there were 'four villagers, three Frenchmen, two riding men, and a priest with two small-holders'. Just under 100 years later the first recorded English fulling mill was in operation at the nearby hamlet of Barton. In 1330 permission was given for a weekly market to be held at Guiting Power, which may explain the current arrangement of the houses about the green. Guiting had its share of the prosperity derived from the 15th-century wool trade, as the addition of the little tower to the church testifies.

Slow to Catch Up

And yet, in other ways, history was slow to catch up with small villages like Guiting. Its farmland, for example, was enclosed only in 1798, allowing small landowners such as a tailor called John Williams, who owned 12 acres (4.86ha) in the form of medieval strips scattered throughout the parish, to finally consolidate their possessions.

Local rights of way were enshrined in law at this time. By the end of the 19th century the rural depression had reduced the population to 431, and it continued to decline throughout the 20th century. Nonetheless, it is recorded that apart from public houses (there were at least four), there were two grocers, two bakers, two tailors, two carpenters, two policemen and a blacksmith.

Local Village for Local People

There are still two pubs in Guiting Power but everything else, apart from the post office and a single grocery store, has disappeared. The village is unusual in that it hasn't succumbed to the inflationary effects of second homeowners from the cities pushing local housing beyond the reach of existing locals. Much of this is down to the far-sightedness of Moya Davidson, a resident in the 1930s, who purchased cottages to be rented out locally. Today these are managed by the Guiting Manor Amenity Trust. It has meant that younger people are able to stay in the village to live and work and there still a few families here who can trace their roots back in Guiting Power for several generations.

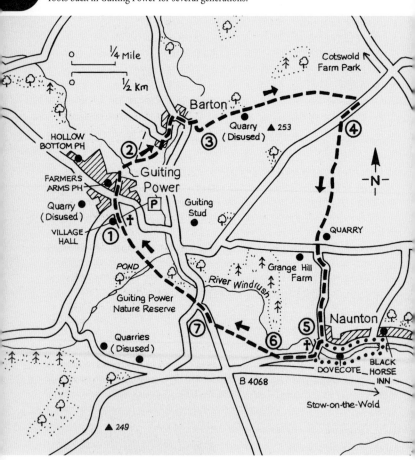

Walk 17 Directions

① From the **village hall** car park walk down the road to the **village green**. Cross the road to walk down a lane. At the bottom go over a stile into a field and turn right. Walk up the bank, up to another stile. Don't cross the one in front of you but clamber over the one to your right into a field.

② Turn left and walk straight across this field to another stile. Cross this and two more to pass a farmhouse in **Barton** village. Follow the lane down to a larger road and turn right. Cross a bridge and turn left up a track and, after 100yds (91m), turn right up another track.

> **WHERE TO EAT AND DRINK**
> Guiting Power's two pubs are the **Farmers Arms**, just off the village green, and the **Hollow Bottom** on the other, Winchcombe, side of the village. Naunton has the very pleasant **Black Horse Inn**.

③ After a few paces bear left and walk along this track for about a mile (1.6km), until you reach another road. Turn right, walk along here for about 250yds (229m) and turn left on to a track.

④ Follow this all the way to a road, passing a **quarry** as you go. Cross the road and enter a lane descending past a house. This quiet lane will bring you all the way into the village of **Naunton**.

> **WHILE YOU'RE THERE** ⓘ
> Located between Guiting Power and Stow-on-the-Wold is the **Cotswold Farm Park**, a sort of zoo specialising in rare breeds of British farm livestock. Animals include the Cotswold 'lion'. This breed of sheep was the foundation of the medieval wool trade and has fortunately been saved from extinction.

⑤ At the junction turn right. Walk through the village and cross the pretty stone bridge by the old mill, passing the old **rectory** to the left and the church concealed to the right. (To get to the Black Horse Inn, turn left and walk along the street for 400yds (366m). Return by entering a drive opposite the pub, turning sharp right over a stile, and

walking back along the side of the river to emerge at a road near the church, where you turn left.) Continue up, out of the village.

⑥ After ¼ mile (400m) turn right over a stile into a field. Turn left, walk to a stile and go into the next field. Cross this field, enter the next one and follow the path to the right of some trees to a gate at the road.

⑦ Turn right along the road and continue to a junction at the bottom. Cross the road to enter a field and walk straight across. At the end go down some steps and pass to the right of a pond. Walk across the next field and then cross a stile to walk to the left of the **church** and return to the start.

> **WHAT TO LOOK FOR** ⓘ
> The Norman doorway in **Guiting church** is an exceptionally rich golden hue. In Naunton, if you stroll back from the Black Horse Inn towards the church on the opposite side of the river then you will be rewarded with a view of a large but charming 17th-century **dovecote**. Many villages had dovecotes for eggs and winter meat.

Woven Charm of Bibury

The outer charm of a weavers' village conceals miserable workings conditions.

•DISTANCE•	6¼ miles (10.1km)
•MINIMUM TIME•	2hrs 30min
•ASCENT / GRADIENT•	165ft (50m) ▲ ▲ ▲
•LEVEL OF DIFFICULTY•	🚶🚶 🚶🚶 🚶🚶
•PATHS•	Fields, tracks and lane, may be muddy in places, 6 stiles
•LANDSCAPE•	Exposed wolds, valley, villages and streams
•SUGGESTED MAP•	aqua3 OS Outdoor Leisure 45 The Cotswolds
•START / FINISH•	Grid reference: SP 113068
•DOG FRIENDLINESS•	On leads throughout – a lot of sheep and horses
•PARKING•	Bibury village
•PUBLIC TOILETS•	Opposite river on main street, close to Arlington Row

BACKGROUND TO THE WALK

Arlington Row is the picturesque terrace of cottages that led William Morris to refer to Bibury as the most beautiful village in England. It was originally built, it is thought, in the late 14th century, to house sheep belonging to Osney Abbey in Oxford. The wool was washed in the river and then hung out to dry on Rack Isle, the marshy area in front of the cottages. Following the dissolution of the monasteries the land was sold off and the sheep houses converted to weavers' cottages. Before mechanisation transformed the wool weaving industry, most weaving took place in the houses of the poor. Firstly, women and children spun the wool either at home or at the workhouse. Then it was transferred to the houses of the weavers, who worked on handlooms at home at piece rates.

A typical weaver's cottage might have had four rooms, with a kitchen and workshop downstairs and a bedroom and storeroom upstairs. There were very few items of furniture in the living rooms, whilst the workroom would have contained little more than a broadloom and the appropriate tools. The woven cloth was then returned to the clothier's mill for fulling and cutting. Work on cloth was often a condition of tenure imposed by landlords. The merchant landlord fixed a piecework rate and, provided that the work was satisfactory, the cottage could stay in the weaver's family from generation to generation. Weaving went on this way for some 200 years, until the introduction of steam power in the 18th century. Consequently it tended to take place in the mills of the Stroud Valley. Despite their unfavourable working conditions, the cottage weavers greatly resisted this change but to no avail – the cottage weaving industry went into inexorable decline.

Strictly speaking, much of what is considered picturesque in Bibury is in the neighbouring village of Arlington, but they are now indistinguishable. Apart from Arlington Row, there is plenty to enjoy in the village, especially the church, which has Saxon origins and is set in pretty gardens. Across the bridge is the old mill, open to the public. Nearby Ablington has an enchantingly pretty group of cottages, threaded by the glittering River Coln. A minor classic, *A Cotswold Village* (1898), which describes local life in the late 19th century, was written by J Arthur Gibbs, the squire who lived at Ablington Manor. You pass the walls of the manor on the walk. Close by, further into the village, are a couple of beautiful 18th-century barns.

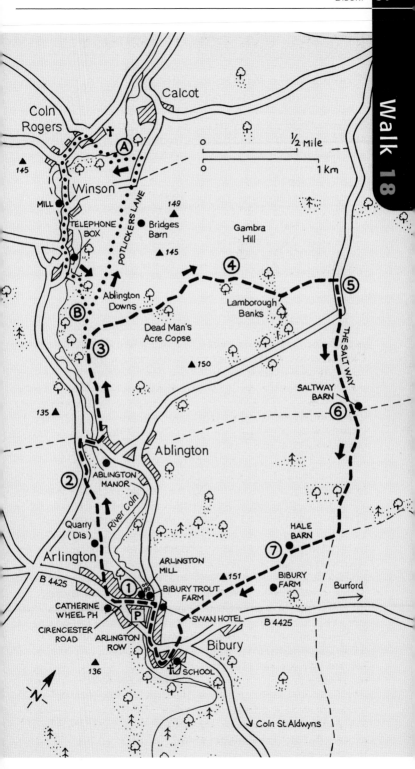

Calcot

Coln Rogers

†

▲ 145

Ⓐ

Winson

MILL

TELEPHONE BOX

POTLICKERS LANE

Bridges Barn

149 ▲

▲ 145

Gambra Hill

Ⓑ

Ablington Downs

Ⓑ

Ⓒ

Ⓓ

Ⓔ

Dead Man's Acre Copse

Lamborough Banks

Ⓓ

Ⓔ

THE SALT WAY

▲ 150

135 ▲

Ⓒ

SALTWAY BARN

Ⓕ

Ablington

ABLINGTON MANOR

River Coln

Ⓑ

Quarry (Dis)

HALE BARN

Arlington

ARLINGTON MILL

Ⓖ

BIBURY FARM

Burford →

①

▲ 151

B 4425

CATHERINE WHEEL PH

P

BIBURY TROUT FARM

SWAN HOTEL

B 4425

CIRENCESTER ROAD

ARLINGTON ROW

Bibury

† SCHOOL

▲ 136

N

↓ Coln St Aldwyns

½ Mile

1 Km

Walk 18 **Directions**

① From the parking area opposite the mill, walk along the **Cirencester road**. Immediately after the **Catherine Wheel** pub turn right along a lane and then keep left at a fork. Pass some cottages and go through gates and stiles into a field. Walk on the same line across several stiles and fields until you pass to the right of a house to a road.

② Turn right and walk down to a junction. Turn right again into **Ablington** and cross the bridge. After a few paces, where the road goes to the right, turn left along a track with houses on your right and a stream to your left. Continue to a gate and then follow the track as it traverses open countryside, arriving at another gate after just over ½ mile (800m).

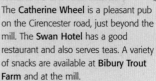

> **WHAT TO LOOK FOR**
> **Ablington Manor** is to your right (behind high stone walls) as you cross the bridge in the village. Look out, too, not just for the 18th-century barns (mentioned above) but also for **Ablington House**, guarded by a pair of lions that once stood at the Houses of Parliament.

③ Go into a field and turn sharp right along the valley bottom (this is where Walk 19 diverges). Follow a twisting route along the bottom of the valley. At the next gate continue into a field, still following the contours of the valley. The route will eventually take you through a gate just before a barn and another immediately after.

④ Keep to the track as it bears right and gently ascends a long slope, with woodland to your left. When the track goes sharp right, with a gate before you, turn left through a gate on to a track. Follow it all the way to a road.

⑤ Turn right. After 250yds (229m), where the road goes right, continue straight on, to enter a track (the **Salt Way**). Continue along this for over ½ mile (800m), until you reach the remains of **Saltway Barn**.

> **WHERE TO EAT AND DRINK** ⓘ
> The **Catherine Wheel** is a pleasant pub on the Cirencester road, just beyond the mill. The **Swan Hotel** has a good restaurant and also serves teas. A variety of snacks are available at **Bibury Trout Farm** and at the mill.

⑥ Do not walk ahead but, immediately after the barns, turn left into a field and then right along its right-hand margin. Walk on for just under ¾ mile (1.2km), passing hedge and woodland and, where the track breaks to the right, turn right through a gate into a field with a wall on your right.

⑦ Walk on to pass to the left of **Hale Barn**. Enter a track, with the large buildings of **Bibury Farm** away to your left, and keep on the same line through gates where they arise. Eventually you will descend to a drive which will, in turn, bring you to a road in **Bibury**. Cross the road to walk down between a row of cottages. At the end, near the church and school, turn right. Walk along the pavement into the village, passing **Arlington Row** and the river on your left.

> **WHILE YOU'RE THERE** ⓘ
> The gardens of **Barnsley House**, home of the late Rosemary Verey, the doyen of modern gardeners, are often open to the public. They are in Barnsley village, on the road to Cirencester.

On to Coln Rogers

This short extension will take you to a pretty part of the broad Coln Valley and two tranquil villages.

See map and information panel for Walk 18

•DISTANCE•	2½ miles (4km)
•MINIMUM TIME•	1hr
•ASCENT / GRADIENT•	213ft (65m)
•LEVEL OF DIFFICULTY•	

Walk 19 Directions (Walk 18 option)

From Point ③ on Walk 18, instead of turning right along the valley, continue up the left side of the field (doing your best to avoid the enormous puddle that is usually there) and ascend to a gate. Go into the next field and keep to its right margin, coming to a gate at the far side. Go through into **Potlickers Lane** and walk along here, passing a farm on your right, all the way to a lane. Turn right along this lane (but do not follow the track on your right) in the direction of **Calcot**.

After 220yds (201m) turn left on to a track, with woodland tumbling away to your right. Ignore a path on your right that will appear soon after you start along here but, after 180yds (165m), turn right down a narrow path that steeples down the bank through the trees, bearing a little to the right.

At the bottom, Point Ⓐ, you will emerge at a path beside the river, with a gate on your left. Turn left, through the gate. Follow the path along the riverbank, with a large house to your left, to cross the river.

Follow the drive to a lane. The interesting **church** on the right along here is of Saxon origin. Continue along the lane to arrive at a junction with a road. Turn left, following the lane through the village of **Coln Rogers**.

Bear left over a bridge and keep going along the road. Later, beside an old **mill**, this road goes sharp right, then left. Continue along the road to reach a junction in **Winson**.

Unusually for a village in the Cotswolds, Winson has several thatched cottages. Turn left and keep left at the village green. The large house overlooking the green was designed by Sir Robert Smirke, the architect responsible for the British Museum.

Stay left, pass a telephone box and walk up a lane for about 100yds (91m). Then go left through a gate and walk down a grassy paddock to another gate. Pass through to cross a bridge and follow a path through a plantation. At the top, Point Ⓑ, turn right with the path and keep going to a gate. In the next field go half left to the far corner. Go through a gate and enter the field back at Point ③. Turn left along the valley floor to continue on Walk 18.

Walk 20

A Haul Around Hazleton and Salperton

An airy walk around quiet villages that owe their existence to medieval trading routes.

·DISTANCE·	5 miles (8km)
·MINIMUM TIME·	2hrs
·ASCENT / GRADIENT·	230ft (70m) ▲▲ ▲ ▲
·LEVEL OF DIFFICULTY·	🚶 🚶 🚶
·PATHS·	Fields (muddy after ploughing), tracks and lanes, no stiles
·LANDSCAPE·	Open wold, small valley, broad views and villages
·SUGGESTED MAP·	aqua3 OS Outdoor Leisure 45 The Cotswolds
·START / FINISH·	Grid reference: SP 080179
·DOG FRIENDLINESS·	Off leads over long, empty stretches of land
·PARKING·	Hazleton village
·PUBLIC TOILETS·	None on route

Walk 20 **Directions**

The walk begins in the southern part of Hazleton, near Priory Farm (the part you will reach first if coming from the A40). Hazleton has a strictly rural feel to it. The village is situated on the route of the ancient Salt Way, which linked the salt workings in Droitwich (between Worcester and Birmingham) with the most convenient, navigable point of the Thames at Lechlade (▶ Walk 5), from where the salt could be transported to London.

Find a signpost to **St Andrew's Church** and take the lane, which passes to the left of it. It has a Norman doorway and a 13th-century font. Much of the region known as the Cotswolds is associated with a stereotypical picture of England: villages made up of impossibly pretty cottages with roses around the door, sleepy

pubs and lazy cricket matches. The picture is not entirely fanciful, but it tends to belie the fact that the area is also characterised by gently undulating hills, or 'wolds', here a Saxon word for open downland.

Leave the village and church behind by continuing on this lane, to reach a junction. Cross this to an obvious farm track opposite. Remain on this to pass to the left of a newer **farmhouse**, crossing a drive and then finding yourself in fields with woodland to your right. Keep going

---

WHILE YOU'RE THERE

Close to the nearby village of Notgrove, about 1½ miles (2.4km) to the north west, is **Notgrove Long Barrow**. Much of it has been removed over the centuries, but nonetheless there is enough left to gain an impression of what it once was like. A little closer to Bourton is **Folly Farm**, a conservation centre that specialises in waterfowl, including various species of goose, duck and chicken.

in the same direction, crossing
several fields and eventually
following the path through
woodland that will bring you to a
gate at a narrow country lane.

The walk continues along the lane
to the right, but at this point you
can, if you wish, turn left and then
very soon right to follow a track to
the church, which stands right
beside **Salperton Park**. This is a
17th-century manor house with
19th-century additions. Walk
through the churchyard, in which
there are several 17th-century table
tombs. Once inside the church, its
most noticeable aspect (to the right
as you enter) is the wall painting
featuring a dancing skeleton
wielding a scythe. There are also
several monuments to the Browne
family; they were, presumably, at
one time the owners of Salperton.
This little village, whose name
derives from its proximity to the
Salt Way, also lies on the ancient
wool-trading trail that linked
Chipping Campden, to the north,
with the southern Cotswolds.

Return to the point where you left
the route and continue along the
lane, passing a copse on your right.
Then, where the hedge on your
right comes to an end, about 150yds
(137m) before a barn, turn right
into a field and walk straight across
it to a gate. Go through this and
strike half left to another gate
leading into the neighbouring field.

The fields here are exceptionally
stony, even by Cotswold standards.
It's easy to understand why
medieval farmers favoured rearing
sheep to the cultivation of crops.

Maintain the same line by going
half right, aiming for a gap in the
wall about half-way down this large
field. Go through and continue in
the same direction across another
field to meet a wall. Turn left to
walk along the side of the field,
with the wall on your right-hand
side. At the bottom turn right on to
a track and walk to the right of a
barn. Continue to a gate and down
a track close to a fence on your
right. Where the field opens up to
the right, carry on down to meet a
fence, which you keep on your right
as it goes a little left to a gate.

It is easy now to see the nature of
wold country: small, sleek hills that
five centuries ago would have been
grazed by thousands of sheep
producing the wool that was the
most highly prized in Europe.

Go through into the field and
follow its right margin, with a
stream running beside you, all the
way to a junction of paths and
tracks. Pass through a gate and turn
right on to a bridleway. Stay on this,
eventually passing through a
farmyard to join the lane – this will
take you back into **Hazleton**.

Larks Above Down Ampney

A route based on the birthplace of one of Britain's best-known composers.

•DISTANCE•	8½ miles (13.7km)
•MINIMUM TIME•	4hrs
•ASCENT / GRADIENT•	100ft (30m) ▲▲▲
•LEVEL OF DIFFICULTY•	🏃 🏃 🏃
•PATHS•	Fields, lanes, tracks, 15 stiles
•LANDSCAPE•	Generally level fields and villages in all directions
•SUGGESTED MAP•	aqua3 OS Explorer 169 Cirencester & Swindon
•START / FINISH•	Grid reference: SU 099965
•DOG FRIENDLINESS•	On leads near livestock but plenty of stretches without
•PARKING•	Down Ampney village
•PUBLIC TOILETS•	None on route

BACKGROUND TO THE WALK

Ralph Vaughan Williams is considered by many to be England's greatest composer. He was born in 1872 in Down Ampney, where his father was vicar, spending the first three years of his life in the Old Vicarage. He studied music in London at the Royal College of Music with Parry, Stanford and Wood, who were the leading British musicians of the day. Then he studied in Berlin with Bruch and later in Paris with Ravel. This experience gave him the confidence to tackle large-scale works, many of which were based on English folk songs, which he had begun to collect in 1903. But Vaughan Williams was also interested in early English liturgical music, the result of which was his *Fantasia on a Theme by Thomas Tallis* (1910) for strings, which combines the English lyrical, pastoral tradition with the stricter demands of early formal composition.

Famous Works

Vaughan Williams went on to compose several symphonies, as well as a ballet based on the ideas of William Blake, and an opera based on *The Pilgrim's Progress* by John Bunyan. There were several sacred works, too, including a Mass and the Revelation oratorio. He also composed the score for the film *Scott of the Antarctic* (1948). One of his best known hymn tunes is *Down Ampney* (1906), named in tribute to his birthplace. For many of us, however, Vaughan Williams is associated with two pieces in particular. The first is his version of *Greensleeves* (1928), the song said to have been originally composed by Henry VIII; and the second is *The Lark Ascending* (1914), the soaring work for violin and orchestra that evokes the poignancy of a bird in flight over the English countryside. Perhaps Williams was thinking of the Cotswolds. He certainly had the Cotswolds in mind when he wrote the opera, *Hugh the Drover* (1924), which is based on traditional folk songs and is set in the village of Northleach at the time of the Napoleonic wars.

There are four Ampneys altogether. Down Ampney church is the finest and definitely worth a visit. It's crowned by a 14th-century spire and contains several interesting effigies. Adjacent to the church is Down Ampney House, a 15th-century manor house that was later redesigned by Sir John Soane. The prettiest of the villages is Ampney Crucis, which takes its name from the 14th-century cross in the churchyard. The head of the cross was only

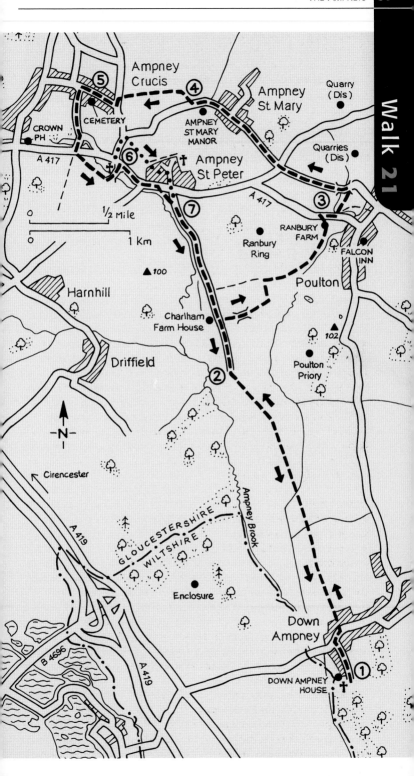

Ampney Crucis

⑤

④

CEMETERY

Ampney St Mary

Quarry (Dis)

CROWN PH

AMPNEY ST MARY MANOR

Quarries (Dis)

A 417

⑥

✝ Ampney St Peter

A 417

③

RANBURY FARM

FALCON INN

⑦

½ Mile

1 Km

Ranbury Ring

Poulton

▲100

Harnhill

Charlham Farm House

Poulton Priory

▲102

②

Driffield

Cirencester

—N—

A 419

GLOUCESTERSHIRE

WILTSHIRE

Ampney Brook

Enclosure

Down Ampney

A 419

B 4696

①

DOWN AMPNEY HOUSE

Walk 21

rediscovered in 1854, having been secreted in the fabric of the church, probably to protect it from puritan zealots in the 16th or 17th century. Ampney St Mary, the second Ampney you come to, is interesting because its original site was abandoned, leaving only the little church you see today. Your route visits the fourth Ampney, Ampney St Peter, before returning to Down Ampney.

Walk 21 Directions

① From the church walk to the centre of the village. At the main road turn right and after 160yds (146m) turn left along a lane. Continue to a track and stay on this to cross a field to woodland.

② Join a track and walk along it to a house. Turn right into a field and on the far side cross a bridge into another field. Cross to a gap and turn left on to a track. At a corner turn right to join a bridleway. Pass through a farmyard to a road.

WHERE TO EAT AND DRINK ℹ️

There are two pubs en route, the **Crown** in Ampney Crucis, and the **Falcon Inn**, just off the route when you get to Poulton. Continue along the road at Point ③ and turn right.

---

③ Turn right. After 200yds (183m) turn left over a stile beside a house. Continue to a second stile, then a stile and footbridge. In the field walk ahead to a stone stile on your left. Cross and walk ahead along a lane to a junction. Follow the lane opposite through **Ampney St Mary**.

④ After the entrance to **Ampney St Mary Manor** on your left, turn right over a stile into a field. Cross this half left to a gate and then turn sharp left to a stile. Cross and walk towards houses. On the far side keep right of a wall and arrive at a stile at a road. Turn left and first right, towards **Ampney Crucis**.

⑤ After a cemetery on the left, turn left down a lane. At the bottom turn right to a main road. Cross to a stile. Enter a field and go quarter left to the river. Find a path leading to a bridge and the churchyard of **Ampney Crucis**. Leave this on the far side and meet the road.

⑥ There are two possibilities here. The shortest is to turn right, pass a lane, then take a footpath on the right. Go half left to a lane and turn right. The other route is longer but avoids traffic. Follow a lane opposite to a junction on your right. Turn right over a stile into a field. Go quarter left to a gate and then immediately right through a gate into a paddock. Cross to another gate and a stile. Go half left to a stile and then, after a few paces, turn right through a gate. Cross a stile and then go half right to a gate. Walk along the margin of a garden and after a stile turn left to emerge in **Ampney St Peter**. Turn right to cross the road and enter a lane.

⑦ Stay on this lane as it becomes a track, from where you retrace your steps to **Down Ampney**.

WHAT TO LOOK FOR ℹ️

In **Down Ampney church** one of the effigies is of a medieval knight in black marble. The small church at Ampney St Mary boasts a complete set of Decorated windows and a Norman lintel over a doorway. In **Ampney St Peter** the churchyard, like Ampney Crucis, contains a 14th-century cross and a small, possibly Saxon, figure near the font.

In Search of King Cod Around Cutsdean and Ford

The origins of the Cotswolds, once the focus of production of England's most valued export.

•DISTANCE•	5½ miles (8.8km)
•MINIMUM TIME•	2hrs 30min
•ASCENT / GRADIENT•	265ft (80m) ▲▲ ▲ ▲
•LEVEL OF DIFFICULTY•	🚶🚶 🚶🚶 🚶
•PATHS•	Tracks, fields and lane, 3 stiles
•LANDSCAPE•	Open wold, farmland, village
•SUGGESTED MAP•	aqua3 OS Outdoor Leisure 45 The Cotswolds
•START / FINISH•	Grid reference: SP 088302
•DOG FRIENDLINESS•	Best on leads – plenty of livestock, including horses
•PARKING•	Cutsdean village
•PUBLIC TOILETS•	None on route

BACKGROUND TO THE WALK

Cutsdean can claim to be the centre of the Cotswolds, according to one theory about the origin of the name 'cotswold'. Today it is nothing more than a small, pretty village on the high, voluptuous wolds above the beginnings of the River Windrush. However, it may once have been the seat of an Anglo-Saxon chief by the name of 'Cod'. His domain would have been his 'dene' and the hilly region in which his domain lay, his 'wolds'. This is plausible, even if there is no verifiable record of a King Cod. Another, possibly more persuasive, explanation concerns the sheep that still graze many hillsides in the Cotswolds, a 'cot' referring to a sheep fold and 'wolds' being the hills that support them. (In Old English a 'cot' is a small dwelling or cottage.)

Lamb's Wool to Lion's Wool

Whatever the truth of the matter, the sheep remain, even if the species that in the Middle Ages produced the finest wool in Europe dwindled to the point of extinction. The ancestors of the 'Cotswold Lion' probably arrived with the Romans, who valued the sheep's milk and their long, dense wool. After the Romans' withdrawal the Saxons continued to farm them; indeed by the 8th century Cotswold fleeces were being exported. The nature of the Cotswolds was perfect for these sheep: the limestone soil produces a calcium-rich diet, good for strong bone growth; and the open, wind-blasted wolds suited this heavy-fleeced breed, able to graze all year long on abundant herbs and grasses. The hills teemed with Cotswold sheep; at one point the Cotswold wool trade accounted for half of England's income.

Distinctive Forelock

It is believed that the medieval Cotswold sheep differed a little from its modern counterpart. Its coat was undoubtedly long and lustrous, but it may have been slightly shorter than that of its descendants. It was the distinctive forelock and the whiteness of its fleece that inspired the nickname, Cotswold Lion, characteristics that persist in the modern sheep.

Under Threat

Why, then, did the fortunes of this miraculous animal plummet? To some extent this is a misconception, since serious decline occurred only with the move to arable farming in the Cotswolds in the mid-20th century. Demand for the wool was strong in the 18th and 19th centuries and the Cotswold was also prized for its meat and its cross-breeding potential. However, the market for long-stapled wool began to decline in favour of finer wool, and crop growing became more attractive to local farmers. Incredibly, by the 1960s, there remained only some 200 animals. Suddenly, it was clear that a living piece of English history was on the verge of extinction. The Cotswold Breed Society was reconvened and steps were taken to ensure the sheep's survival. Farmers have since rediscovered the animal's many qualities, and it is no longer quite such a rare sight on the wolds.

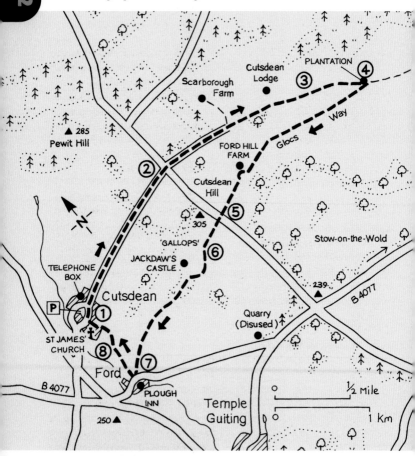

Walk 22 Directions

① With the **Church of St James** to your right-hand side and, after a few paces, a telephone box away to your left, walk out of the village of

Cutsdean. Continue uphill on this straight country road for just over a mile (1.6km), until you come to a T-junction with another road.

② Cross this to enter another lane, at the margin of **woodland**. Emerge from the woods, and, where the track veers left towards a house, keep straight on.

③ Eventually you will come to a field. Walk straight on for 200yds (183m) and then go quarter right over the brow of a slope to head for a **plantation**.

④ Pass through the plantation. At a junction turn right and right again, the plantation now on your right. Follow this track – passing through the precincts of **Ford Hill Farm** – all the way to a road.

⑤ Cross over, to enter a track which runs to the left of a 'gallops', used for training racehorses. Keep straight on where the track veers left into a neighbouring field. Shortly after this the track becomes a metalled lane, still running alongside the gallops.

⑥ Soon after passing the stables of **Jackdaw's Castle** across to your right, you need to turn sharp right across the gallops area (watch out for horses) to join a track, where you turn left. The track descends gently for just under a mile (1.6km), the gallops and greensward to your left. Keep descending until you are near the bottom, at the beginning of a

> **WHERE TO EAT AND DRINK** ⓘ
> The route passes close to the old and very attractive **Plough Inn** in Ford. It serves Donnington's, the local beer brewed in a charming lakeside brewery near Stow-on-the-Wold. The nearest towns with a greater choice are Winchcombe and Stow.

village. This is **Ford**: if you walk into the village you will see the welcoming **Plough Inn** directly in front of you.

⑦ Otherwise turn right, right again and then left, to walk along a grassy path between railings. On the far side turn right, with the railings to your right, and soon arrive at a bank. Follow the path down among trees as it bears left to a stile.

> **WHILE YOU'RE THERE** ⓘ
> The **Cotswold Farm Park**, which contributed much to the conservation of the Cotswold Lion, is only a short drive to the south. Established over 30 years ago, it is one of the few places in the country where you can still see native breeds of domestic animals and birds, many of which have been brought close to extinction by modern developments in farming practice. As well as a café and a shop there is a school for tractor driving.

⑧ Cross into a field and then go half right across it. Go down a bank, across a rivulet (possibly dried up in summertime) and up the bank on the other side to a stile. Cross into a field and turn left along the side of the field towards **Cutsdean**. Pass to the right of the church, which sits back across a wall to your left. At the edge of the village come to a stile: cross this to join a track. After a few paces emerge on to the **main street** through the village and your starting point.

> **WHAT TO LOOK FOR** ⓘ
> Horses are very important to the local economy. The countryside is covered in 'gallops', earthy tracks where racehorses can be exercised in safety. You'll also notice a large number of jumps, like the hurdles at a proper race course. Many racehorses are bred here, and some may get to race at nearby Cheltenham, home to the pre-eminent steeplechase course in the country and host to the huge Cheltenham Festival racing event.

Walk 23

From Snowshill

Three of Gloucestershire's finest villages, saved from decline and decay.

•DISTANCE•	6¼ miles (10.1km)
•MINIMUM TIME•	2hrs 45min
•ASCENT / GRADIENT•	625ft (190m) ▲▲▲
•LEVEL OF DIFFICULTY•	🚶🚶 🚶🚶 🚶
•PATHS•	Tracks, estate grassland and pavement
•LANDSCAPE•	High grassland, open wold, wide-ranging views and villages
•SUGGESTED MAP•	aqua3 OS Outdoor Leisure 45 The Cotswolds
•START / FINISH•	Grid reference: SP 096337
•DOG FRIENDLINESS•	On leads – livestock on most parts of walk
•PARKING•	Snowshill village
•PUBLIC TOILETS•	None on route

BACKGROUND TO THE WALK

The villages of the Cotswolds are radiant examples of English vernacular architecture, but they have not always been the prosperous places they are today. Many, like Stanton and Snowshill, were once owned by the great abbeys. With the dissolution of the monasteries they became the property of private landlords. Subsistence farmers were edged out by the introduction of short leases and enclosure. Villagers who had farmed their own strips of land became labourers. The number of small farmers decreased dramatically and, with the innovations of the Industrial Revolution, so too did the demand for labour. Cheaper food flooded in from overseas and several catastrophic harvests compounded the problem.

People left the countryside in droves to work in the industrial towns and cities. Cotswold villages, once at the core of the most important woollen industry in medieval Europe, became impoverished backwaters. But the villages themselves resisted decay. Unlike villages in many other parts of Britain, their buildings were made of stone. Enlightened landlords, who cherished their innate beauty, turned them into huge restoration projects.

The three villages encountered on this walk are living reminders of this process. Snowshill, together with Stanton, was once owned by Winchcombe Abbey. In 1539 it became the property of Henry VIII's sixth wife, Catherine Parr. The manor house was transformed into the estate's administrative centre and remained in the Parr family until 1919. Then the estate was bought by Charles Wade, a sugar plantation owner. He restored the house and devoted his time to amassing an extraordinary collection of art and artefacts, which he subsequently bequeathed to the National Trust. Now forming the basis of a museum, his collection, from Japanese armour to farm machinery, is of enormous appeal. Next on this walk comes Stanway, a small hamlet at the centre of a large estate owned by Lord Neidpath. The most striking feature here is the magnificent gatehouse to the Jacobean Stanway House, a gem of Cotswold architecture built around 1630.

Stanton comes last. It was rescued from oblivion in 1906 by the architect Sir Philip Stott. He bought and restored Stanton Court and many of the village's 16th-century houses. The peaceful parish church is located along a lane leading from the market cross. It has two pulpits (one dating from the 14th-century, the other Jacobean) and the founder of Methodism, John Wesley, preached here in 1733.

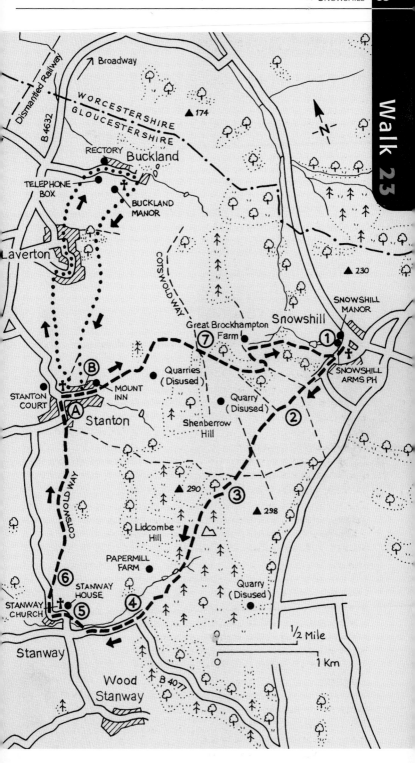

Broadway

WORCESTERSHIRE
GLOUCESTERSHIRE

Dismantled Railway

B 4632

▲ 174

RECTORY Buckland

TELEPHONE
BOX

BUCKLAND MANOR

Laverton

▲ 230

COTSWOLD WAY

SNOWSHILL
MANOR

Great Brockhampton
Farm

⑦ Snowshill

①

B

Quarries
(Disused)

MOUNT
INN

SNOWSHILL
ARMS PH

STANTON
COURT

A

Stanton

Quarry
(Disused)

②

Shenberrow
Hill

COTSWOLD WAY

▲ 290

③

▲ 298

Lidcombe
Hill

⑥

PAPERMILL
FARM

STANWAY
HOUSE

Quarry
(Disused)

STANWAY
CHURCH ⑤

④

½ Mile

1 Km

Stanway

Wood
STANWAY

B 4077

Walk 23 Directions

① Walk out of Snowshill village with the **church** on your left. After ¼ mile (400m) turn right, down a lane. After another ¼ mile (400m), at a corner, turn left up to a gate and enter a field.

② Go quarter left to a gate. In the next field go half right to the far corner and left along a track. Take the second footpath on the right through a gate into a field and walk across to another field. Cross this to a track.

WHAT TO LOOK FOR ℹ

As you pass through Stanway, look to the left before you mount the stile. You'll see the cricket pitch and, overlooking it, a **thatched pavilion**. This was presented to Stanway at the beginning of the 20th century by J M Barrie, creator of Peter Pan, a keen cricketer and a regular visitor to Stanway House.

---

③ Walk down the track. After 275yds (251m) turn right on to a stony track, descending steeply through **Lidcombe Wood**. Where it flattens out a farm will come into view across fields to the right, after which the track bears left. Continue straight on along a narrow footpath to a road.

④ Walk along the pavement and, after 500yds (457m), turn right over a stile into a small **orchard**. Walk across this, bearing slightly right, to arrive at a gate. Go through and walk with a high wall to your right, to a road.

⑤ Turn right and pass the impressive entrance to **Stanway House** and **Stanway church**. Follow the road as it goes right. Shortly

after another entrance turn right over a stile. Go half left to another stile and in the next large field go half right.

⑥ Now walk all the way into **Stanton**, following the regular and clear waymarkers of the Cotswold Way. After 1 mile (1.6km) you will arrive at a stile at the edge of Stanton. Turn left along a track to a junction. Turn right here and walk through the village. Where the road goes left, walk straight on, passing the stone cross (Point Ⓐ) and then another footpath (Point Ⓑ). Climb up to pass the **Mount Inn**. Behind it walk up a steep, shaded path to a gate. Then walk straight up the hill (ignoring a path to the right after a few paces). Climb all the way to the top to meet a lane.

⑦ Walk down the lane for 250yds (229m) then turn left over a stile into woodland. Follow the path, going left at a fork. At the bottom cross a stile on to a lane and turn left. Walk along here for 200yds (183m). Before a cottage turn right over a stile into a scrubby field. Cross to the far side and turn right through a gate. Continue to a stile on your right, cross it and turn left. Follow the margin of this grassy area to a gate and then follow the path back into **Snowshill**.

WHILE YOU'RE THERE ℹ

Even those who usually shun museums should make an exception for the one at **Snowshill Manor**, which is more like a fantastical toyshop than a museum. Although the manor is near the heart of the village, the entrance is outside it, on the Broadway road. **Stanway House** has restricted opening hours but is similarly worth a visit – anything less like the conventional picture of a stately home is hard to imagine.

Laverton and Buckland

Embrace two more gorgeous villages by extending Walk 23.
See map and information panel for Walk 23

•DISTANCE•	9 miles (14.5km)
•MINIMUM TIME•	3hrs
•ASCENT / GRADIENT•	675ft (205m) ▲ ▲ ▲
•LEVEL OF DIFFICULTY•	👫 👫 👫

Walk 24 Directions (Walk 23 option)

From **Stanton war memorial** (Point Ⓐ) head for the **churchyard**, passing to the right of the church. In the corner turn right along an alley. At the end turn left and follow a path to a gate. Cross a plank bridge to a field and bear left, to reach a stile in a gap. Cross and turn right. At the next corner cross a bridge stile and continue to another stile. Walk ahead, go over a stile just to the left of the corner and continue towards **Laverton**, a large hamlet liberally stocked with Cotswold stone architecture. Aim to the left of a house and turn right at the road. Follow the road through Laverton as it goes left, left and right. At a junction beside a tree with a seat, cross to enter a firm bridleway. Follow this to the main street of **Buckland**. Turn right and walk through the village. Shortly after a telephone box and a footpath

> **WHERE TO EAT AND DRINK** ⓘ
> There are two pubs on the route: the **Snowshill Arms** in Snowshill and the **Mount Inn** in Stanton. Both are welcoming and serve good food. There is also a **tea room** a little beyond where you leave the road to walk into Stanway.

sign you will see, on your left, the 15th-century rectory – the oldest medieval parsonage in Gloucestershire still in use. It has some fine stained glass and a timbered great hall. The 18th-century founder of Methodism, John Wesley, often used it as a base. Shortly, to your right, is the church.

At the top, where the road curves left, go straight on to a kissing gate. Go through to a field and turn right. Pass handsome **Buckland Manor** (now a hotel) on the right. The neighbouring church contains medieval glass restored by William Morris, and a painted panel originally in Hailes Abbey. Go through another two kissing gates, then through a bridle gate and continue straight on. Pass through some trees to a gate. Stay on this same line, passing through a series of gates and stiles. You'll come to a large field on the flank of the hill. Follow markers here and, after ¼ mile (400m), cross a stile beside a gate. Continue until the path appears to divide after a string of trees. Take the higher option and walk on a wide path between trees and bushes. Go over a stile and walk straight ahead until you come to a stile at the edge of **Stanton**. Go through and walk into the village centre, Point Ⓑ.

Walk 25

Around Chedworth Villa

Finding out how wealthy Romanised Britons lived in the Cotswolds.

•DISTANCE•	4½ miles (7.2km)
•MINIMUM TIME•	2hrs
•ASCENT / GRADIENT•	310ft (95m) 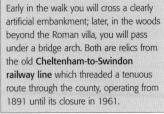
•LEVEL OF DIFFICULTY•	
•PATHS•	Tracks, lanes, fields and woodland, 8 stiles
•LANDSCAPE•	Meadows, streams, woods and shallow valleys
•SUGGESTED MAP•	aqua3 OS Outdoor Leisure 45 The Cotswolds
•START / FINISH•	Grid reference: SP 052121
•DOG FRIENDLINESS•	Quite good – plenty of quiet lanes and tracks
•PARKING•	Car park in front of Chedworth church (restricted to congregation during services)
•PUBLIC TOILETS•	None on route

Walk 25 Directions

From **Chedworth church** go through a gate to the right of the **Seven Tuns** pub. Walk to the right of the stables and go over a stile into a field. Now walk across this field and locate a stile in front of you, to the left of a gate. Cross this and almost immediately turn left over another stile into woodland.

The subject of this walk, the Chedworth Roman Villa, sits in a secluded, wooded stretch of the Coln valley, well protected from the elements and with a good supply of water – the spring later fed a temple to a water goddess. Despite our usual perception of a historically densely wooded Britain, the truth is that the villa would have stood in open countryside.

Follow a path up to cross the route of the **old railway line** and then down the other side, bearing left, to bring you to a stile on your right. Go over into a field and walk down

this to cross another stile. Take a stone slab across a stream then bear left up to a lane. Cross the lane and then, keeping left of the cottages, go up to a gate. Go on up the field to another gate and walk along a path ahead, passing through two more gates to arrive at a lane.

WHAT TO LOOK FOR ⓘ

Early in the walk you will cross a clearly artificial embankment; later, in the woods beyond the Roman villa, you will pass under a bridge arch. Both are relics from the old **Cheltenham-to-Swindon railway line** which threaded a tenuous route through the county, operating from 1891 until its closure in 1961.

Turn right here and walk along the lane for 600yds (549m), passing barns on the left. When you reach a point where there are footpaths to the left and right, turn left into a field and walk dead ahead, passing just left of a pair of trees and down beyond, to the edge of **woodland**.

Follow a track through the woods for 550yds (503m). Then, at a

Walk 25

marker, go diagonally left up to a track and turn right. After a few paces turn left on a path that will soon bring you down to a road. Turn left here and, at a sharp corner, with **Yanworth Mill** to your right, walk straight on to enter a track. Follow this until it comes to an end at a road. Turn left and walk on to arrive at the **Roman villa**.

Although it was eventually the home of a well-to-do family, to begin with the villa functioned primarily as a farmhouse. The surrounding land was used for cultivating crops and raising animals. The resulting produce was distributed along the nearby Fosse Way. It was 200 years later that Chedworth was turned into the villa of a rich family. Steam baths were added and the common rooms were enlarged. The beautiful mosaic floors were laid down in the last part of the 4th century AD. It is believed that the occupants of the villa, in either of its incarnations, were almost certainly not from Rome – it is more likely that they were native people who had thrown in their lot with the new rulers.

The Romans invaded Britain in AD 43 and appeared to have brought the area that is now Gloucestershire under their thrall within four years. The area west of the Fosse Way remained under military alert for another decade, but by AD 60 the Romans were established as rulers.

The process of colonisation was a long one, but by the early part of the 2nd century AD the Romans and their subjects, known as the 'Romano-British', felt sufficiently at ease to begin the construction of small, timber-framed villas in the valleys of the Cotswold escarpment. Later ones were built of stone, but the features that have survived best in the centuries since are the magnificent mosaics that were made by craftsmen from Cirencester, which was the second town of Roman Britain. Even though the Roman administration withdrew from Britain in AD 410, mosaics were still being constructed as late as AD 395. Chedworth, however, is an early example, dating from about AD 120.

Carry on past the villa and enter **woodland**. Pass beneath an old **railway bridge** and continue to a crossroads of tracks. Turn left here and follow the main track until it takes you out of the woods, bringing you to a stile at the edge of a field. Walk across this until you reach a selection of gates at a corner. Take the gate in front of you and continue ahead, soon to descend quite steeply to a stile at the edge of a field. Now walk ahead across this field until, just before a cottage on the right, you turn right to a stile beside it. Cross this and follow the lane back to the start.

Around the Lakes of the Cotswold Water Park

Through an evolving landscape in the southern Cotswolds.

•DISTANCE•	5 miles (8km)
•MINIMUM TIME•	2hrs
•ASCENT / GRADIENT•	Negligible
•LEVEL OF DIFFICULTY•	
•PATHS•	Track, tow path and lanes, 10 stiles
•LANDSCAPE•	Dead flat – lakes, light woodland, canal and village
•SUGGESTED MAP•	aqua3 OS Explorer 169 Cirencester & Swindon
•START / FINISH•	Grid reference: SU 048974
•DOG FRIENDLINESS•	Good but be aware of a lot of waterfowl around lakes
•PARKING•	Silver Street, South Cerney
•PUBLIC TOILETS•	None on route

BACKGROUND TO THE WALK

By their very nature, ancient landscapes and historic architecture evolve very slowly, changing little from one century to another. Can they resist the demands of a brasher era? In the Cotswolds the answer to this question is essentially 'yes'. Here building restrictions are strict – even, sometimes, draconian. The result, however, is a significant area of largely unspoilt English countryside; sometimes, thoughtful development has even enhanced an otherwise lacklustre skyline. The Cotswold Water Park, located in and around old gravel pits, is an example of this.

Recreational Gravel

Gravel has been worked in the upper Thames Valley, where the water table is close to the surface, since the 1920s. The removal of gravel leads to the creation of lakes and in the areas around South Cerney and between Fairford and Lechlade there are now some 4,000 acres (1,620ha) of water, in about 100 lakes. They provide an important wetland habitat for a variety of wildlife. Most of these lakes have been turned over to recreational use of one sort or another, being a perfect place for game and coarse fishing, board sailing, walking, boating of various kinds, riding and sundry other leisure activities. Interestingly, this has been what is now called a private/public enterprise. The landscaping has not just been a case of letting nature take over where the gravel excavators left off. The crane-grabs that were used for excavation in the 1960s, for example, left the gravel pits with vertical sides and therefore with deep water right up to the shoreline. As it happens, some forms of aquatic life flourish under these conditions, but in other lakes the shoreline has been graded to create a gentler slope – this harmonises better with the essentially flat landscape in this part of the Cotswolds and is better suited to the needs of swimmers and children. In the same way, trees have been planted and artificial hills have been constructed to offer both shelter and visual relief. Old brick railway bridges have been preserved. Finally, a style of waterside architecture has been developed to attract people to live here. It continues to evolve, just as the surrounding countryside has done for centuries.

South Cerney & Cerney Wick

The walk begins in South Cerney, by the River Churn, only 4 miles (6.4km) from the source of the Thames. Look inside the Norman church for the exceptional carving on the 12th-century rood. Later the walk takes you through Cerney Wick, a smaller village on the other side of the gravel workings. The highlight here is an 18th-century 'roundhouse', used by the workers on the now disued Thames and Severn Canal.

Walk 26

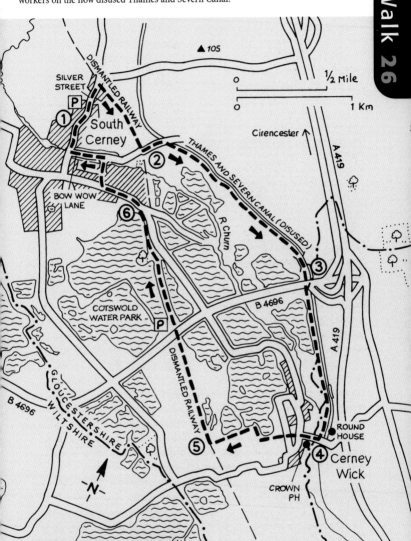

Walk 26 Directions

① From **Silver Street** walk north out of the village. Immediately before the turning to Driffield and

Cricklade, turn right over a stile on to a bank. Stay on this obvious path for 800yds (732m), to reach a brick bridge across the path. Turn right here up a flight of steps to reach a narrow road.

② Turn left and walk along here for 200yds (183m) until you come to footpaths to the right and left. Turn right along a farm track, following a signpost for **Cerney Wick**. Almost immediately the shallow, overgrown remains of the **Thames and Severn Canal** appear to your left. When the track veers right into a farm, walk ahead over a stile to follow a path beneath the trees – the old canal tow path. At a bridge keep ahead across stiles and continue until you come to a busy road.

> **WHILE YOU'RE THERE** ⓘ
> Visit often-overlooked **Cricklade**. The town centre is dominated by 17th- and 18th-century houses, overseen by the bulky tower of the church, visible for miles around. Unusually, it is dedicated to the Breton St Samson.

> **WHERE TO EAT AND DRINK** ⓘ
> The walk passes the **Crown** in Cerney Wick. There are also several pubs in South Cerney – the **Old George** and the **Eliot Arms** in Clarks Hay, and the **Royal Oak** on the High Street.

③ Cross with care. On the far side you have two choices: either continue on the tow path or take the path that skirts the lakes. If you take the lakeside path, you will eventually be able to rejoin the tow path by going left at a bridge after 600yds (549m). Continue until, after just under ½ mile (800m), you pass an old canal roundhouse across the canal to the left and, soon after, reach a lane at **Cerney Wick**.

④ Turn right here and walk to the junction at the end of the road, beside the **Crown** pub. Cross to a

stile and enter a field. Walk straight ahead and come to another stile. Cross this aiming to the left of a cottage. Cross the lane, go over another stile and enter a field. Walk ahead and follow the path as it guides you across a stile on to the grass by a lake. Walk around the lake, going right and then left. In the corner before you, cross into a field, walk ahead towards trees and cross a stile to a track.

⑤ Turn right, rejoining the **old railway line** and following it all the way to a road. Cross this into a car park and go through a gate on to a track. Stay on this all the way to another road and follow a path that runs to its left.

⑥ Where the path ends at the beginning of **South Cerney**, continue along **Station Road**. Ignore a footpath on the right but turn right at the second one, which takes you across a bridge and brings you to a lane called '**Bow Wow**'. Turn left here between streams and return to **Silver Street**.

> **WHAT TO LOOK FOR** ⓘ
> Disused **transport systems** feature greatly in this walk. For much of it you will be beside or close to the old Thames and Severn Canal (▶ Walk 33), or following the route of the old Andoversford railway line. The line linked Cheltenham and Swindon between 1891 and 1961. The **roundhouse** seen on the far side of the old canal as you approach Cerney Wick was used by lock keepers and maintenance engineers. This design was a distinctive feature of the Thames and Severn Canal. Even the windows were rounded to afford the occupants maximum visibility of their stretch of canal. The downstairs would have been used as a stable, the middle storey as a living area and the upstairs held sleeping accomodation. The flat roof was also put to use collecting rainwater for the house's water supply.

Thomas Cromwell and the Destruction of Hailes Abbey

How an important abbey was destroyed by a King's Commissioner.

·DISTANCE·	5 miles (8km)
·MINIMUM TIME·	2hrs
·ASCENT / GRADIENT·	605ft (185m) ▲ ▲ ▲
·LEVEL OF DIFFICULTY·	🏃 🏃 🏃
·PATHS·	Fields, tracks, farmyard and lanes, 7 stiles
·LANDSCAPE·	Wide views, rolling wolds and villages
·SUGGESTED MAP·	aqua3 OS Outdoor Leisure 45 The Cotswolds
·START / FINISH·	Grid reference: SP 050301
·DOG FRIENDLINESS·	Mostly on leads – a lot of livestock in fields
·PARKING·	Beside Hailes church
·PUBLIC TOILETS·	None on route

BACKGROUND TO THE WALK

In the decade from 1536 to 1547 just about every English religious institution that was not a parish church was either closed or destroyed – this was the Dissolution, Henry VIII's draconian policy to force the old Church to give up its enormous wealth. The smaller monasteries went first, then the larger ones and finally the colleges and chantries. All their lands and tithes became Crown property. Much of them were sold off to laypeople, usually to local, influential landowners. The Church as a parish institution was considerably strengthened as a result of the Dissolution, but at the expense of the wider religious life. The suppression of the chantries and guilds, for example, meant that many people were deprived of a local place of worship.

Hailes Abbey

Hailes Abbey was one of the most powerful Cistercian monasteries in the country, owning 13,000 acres (5,265ha) and 8,000 sheep. It was a particular target for reformers. In 1270 Edmund, Earl of Cornwall, the son of its founder, had given the monastery a phial supposed to contain the blood of Christ. Thomas Cromwell was the King's Commissioner responsible for seeing to the closure of the monasteries. He is reputed to have surveyed the destruction of the monastery from a vantage point near Beckbury Camp. There is still a fine view of the abbey from here, as you should find as you pass Point ⑤ on this walk. According to Hugh Latimer of Worcester, who had been working with him, Cromwell also spent an afternoon in 1539 examining the so-called 'blood'. Cromwell concluded that it was nothing more than an 'unctuous gum and compound of many things'. Once the valuables had been removed, local people took what was left.

The monastery lands were disposed of in a typical manner. First they were confiscated by the Crown and then sold to a speculator who sold the land on in lots. In about 1600 the site of the abbey was bought by Sir John Tracy, the builder of Stanway House. The monks were dispersed: a few managed to secure positions as part of the parish clergy, whilst others took up posts with the cathedrals at Bristol and Gloucester. Others returned to the laity.

Charming Remains

Hailes church is all that remains of the village of Hailes. It predates the abbey and survived the Dissolution, perhaps because it had been a parish church and was not directly linked to the neighbouring monastery. It is a church of real charm, sadly ignored by the many visitors to the monastery's ruins. Although very small, it has several special features, including a panelled chancel – floored with tiles from the monastery – and a nave with 14th-century wall paintings. Didbrook church also survived the upheavals. Built in Perpendicular style, it was rebuilt in 1475 by the Abbot of Hailes, following damage caused by Lancastrian soldiers after the Battle of Tewkesbury.

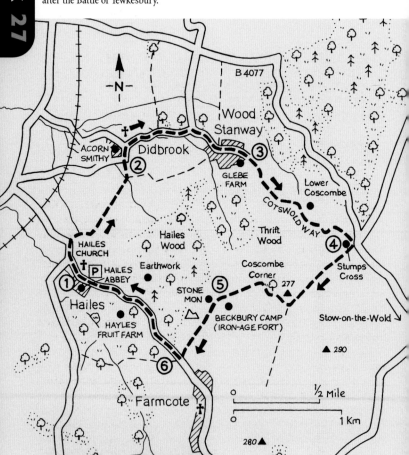

Walk 27 Directions

① From **Hailes church** turn right and follow the lane to a T-junction. Turn right and after 200yds (183m) turn right on to a footpath. Cross an area of concrete and follow a track as it goes right and left, becoming a grassy path beside a field. Go through a gate, followed by a stile. After about 75yds (69m) turn left, through a gate, and cross a field to a gate at a road.

② Turn right and follow the road as it meanders through the pretty village of **Didbrook** then a stretch

Walk 27

of countryside. At a junction turn
right for **Wood Stanway**. Walk
through this village into the yard of
Glebe Farm.

③ At a gate and a stile cross into a
field and walk ahead, looking for a
stile on the left. You are now on the
Cotswold Way, well marked by
arrows with a white dot or acorn.
Cross into a field and go half right,
keeping to the left of some
telegraph poles, to a gap in a hedge.
Bear half left across the next field,
heading towards a house. Cross a
stile and turn sharp right, up the
slope, to a stile on your right. Cross
this and turn immediately left up
the field. Go left over a ladder stile
by a gate. Follow the footpath as it
wends its way gently up the slope.
At the top go straight ahead to a
gate at a road.

④ Turn right and right again
through a gate to a track. Follow
this, passing through a gate, until at
the top (just before some trees), you
turn right to follow another track
for 50yds (46m). Turn left through
a gate into a field and turn sharp

right to follow the perimeter of the
field as it goes left and passes
through a gate beside the ramparts
of an Iron-Age fort, **Beckbury
Camp**. Continue ahead to pass
through another gate which leads to
a stone monument with a niche.
According to local lore, this is the
point from where Thomas
Cromwell watched the destruction
of Hailes Abbey in 1539.

⑤ Turn right to follow a steep path
down through the trees. At the
bottom go straight across down the
field to a gate. Pass through,
continue down to another gate and,
in the field beyond, head down to a
stile beside a signpost.

⑥ Cross this and turn right down a
lane, all the way to a road. To the
left is **Hayles Fruit Farm** with its
café. Continue ahead along the road
to return to **Hailes Abbey** and the
starting point by the church.

Winchcombe and Sudeley Castle

A walk above the burial place of Henry's sixth queen – Catherine Parr.

•DISTANCE•	4 miles (6.4km)
•MINIMUM TIME•	2hrs
•ASCENT / GRADIENT•	490ft (150m) ▲▲▲
•LEVEL OF DIFFICULTY•	斧 斧 斧
•PATHS•	Fields and lanes, 10 stiles
•LANDSCAPE•	Woodland, hills and villages
•SUGGESTED MAP•	aqua3 OS Outdoor Leisure 45 The Cotswolds
•START / FINISH•	Grid reference: SP 024282
•DOG FRIENDLINESS•	On leads (or close control) throughout – much livestock
•PARKING•	Free on Abbey Terrace; also car park on Back Lane
•PUBLIC TOILETS•	On corner of Vine Street

BACKGROUND TO THE WALK

At the end of a long drive just outside Winchcombe is a largely 16th-century mansion called Sudeley Castle. The first castle was built here in 1140 and fragments dating from its earlier, more martial days are still much in evidence. Originally little more than a fortified manor house, by the mid-15th century it had acquired a keep and several courtyards. It became a royal castle after the Wars of the Roses before being given to Thomas Seymour, Edward VI's Lord High Admiral. Seymour lived at Sudeley with his wife, Catherine Parr – he was her fourth husband. Seymour was executed for treason. Consequently the castle passed to Catherine's brother, William, but he was executed too. Queen Mary gave the property to Sir John Brydges, the first Lord Chandos. Sudeley Castle was a Royalist stronghold during the Civil War. It was disarmed by the Parliamentarians and left to decay until its purchase by the wealthy Dent brothers in 1863.

Married at Nine Years Old

Catherine Parr, sixth wife of Henry VIII and the only one to outlive him, is buried in Sudeley's chapel. She was born in 1512 into an influential northern family and educated in Henry's court. She was first married at the tender age of nine, but widowed six years later. Back at court, she was at the centre of a group of educated, capable women, using her influence with the King to protect her second husband, Lord Latimer, from the machinations of courtly politics. When Latimer died in 1543, Catherine was left one of the wealthiest and best-connected women in England, and an obvious choice of wife for Henry. She looked after him and his affairs during the years until his death in 1547. She quickly married Seymour and moved to Sudeley, where the future Queen Elizabeth was often her companion until Catherine's death in childbirth in 1548.

The village of Winchcombe has a considerable history. It was a seat of the Mercian kings and the capital of Winchcombshire until its incorporation into Gloucestershire in the 11th century. It became a significant place of pilgrimage due to the presence of an abbey established in AD 798 and dedicated to St Kenelm, the son of its founder, King Kenulf. The abbey was razed in the Dissolution but the parish church survived and is a fine example of a 'wool church', financed through income from the medieval wool trade. Of particular interest are the amusing gargoyles that decorate its exterior. They are said to be modelled on real local people. Winchcombe also boasts two stimulating small museums: the Folk Museum on the corner of North Street and the Railway Museum on Gloucester Street. Unlike many villages in the area, it has has retained many of its shops and local services.

Walk 28

Walk 28 Directions

① From the parking area on **Abbey Terrace** in Winchcombe, walk towards the village centre and turn right, down **Castle Street**. Where it levels out cross a bridge and after a few paces turn left on a path between cottages. Pass into a field and go half right to a gate on the other side.

WHAT TO LOOK FOR ⓘ

If you go into the church at Winchcombe, note the **embroidery** behind a screen, said to be the work of Catherine of Aragon, a wife of Henry VIII. As you descend the hill on the approach to Sudeley Hill Farm, look out for **St Kenelm's Well**. This is a 19th-century version of a holy well connected with the martyred prince, patron saint of the vanished Winchcombe Abbey.

② Turn right along a lane. At the end of a high stone wall to your right, turn left into a field. Go half right across this field to find a well-concealed gap in the hedge, about 50yds (46m) left of a gateway, with a plank across a ditch. Cross this and then turn left to a gate. Go through and continue half right to another gap in the hedge. Pass through and maintain your direction to a protruding corner. Once you are round it, keep close to the fence on your left and continue into the next corner to find a (possibly overgrown) path leading to a stile.

③ Cross the next field to another stile. Continue up the following field to a gate. Go through and then go half right to the far corner to another stile, again possibly

WHILE YOU'RE THERE ⓘ

In Winchcombe itself you should try and visit **Sudeley Castle**, the **parish church** and the two **museums** (► Background to the Walk). Just outside the town, on the road to Stanway, is **Toddington Station**, and the Gloucestershire & Warwickshire Railway. Here enthusiasts are aiming to reopen the old Great Western Railway route between Stratford-upon-Avon and Cheltenham. Steam train services operate at weekends over their 6½ miles (10.4km) of restored track between Toddington and Gotherington.

concealed. Cross this and then another stile almost immediately. Continue until you come to a stile beside a gate with a stone barn above you to the right.

④ Don't go over the stile but turn right to head downhill to a gate (at first hidden) in the hedge about 250yds (229m) below the barn. Go through this on to a track and follow it as it curves towards a house. Cross a stile.

⑤ Just before the house turn right, cross the field and go over a stile. In the next field go to the bottom left-hand corner to emerge on a road. Turn left and, after a few paces, turn right along a lane, towards **Sudeley Lodge Parks Farm**.

WHERE TO EAT AND DRINK ⓘ

For a small town, **Winchcombe** has a disproportionately large number of possibilities, ranging from pubs to tea rooms and restaurants. It also has a bakery (and a supermarket). If you visit **Sudeley Castle**, there's a good café.

⑥ Opposite a cottage turn right on to a footpath across a field. At the bottom nip over a stile and turn right. At the next corner turn left, remaining in the same field. Cross another stile, continue for a few paces and then turn right over a stile. Walk half left, following the obvious waymarkers to a fence, with **Sudeley Castle** now on your right-hand side.

⑦ Go through two kissing gates to enter the park area. Cross a drive and then cross a field to another gate. Go through this and bear half right to the farthest corner. You will emerge on **Castle Street** in Winchcombe where you can turn left to return to the village centre.

On to Belas Knap

Extend Walk 28 by visiting a well-preserved neolithic barrow.
See map and information panel for Walk 28

•DISTANCE•	7¾ miles (12.5km)
•MINIMUM TIME•	3hrs 30min
•ASCENT / GRADIENT•	1,017ft (310m) ▲▲▲
•LEVEL OF DIFFICULTY•	🚶🚶 🚶🚶 🚶

Walk 29 Directions (Walk 28 option)

The Cotswolds are riddled with settlement remains from all eras, including early tombs. Of these, the huge green mound of Belas Knap, which means 'beacon hill', is the most evocative. It stands in a field overlooking Winchcombe.

From Point Ⓐ turn left to follow the drive all the way to a **lodge** and a road. Turn left. After 300yds (274m) go through a kissing gate on the right. Go half left to a stile and cross two further fields on the same line. In the far corner of the third field cross a footbridge to a field and follow its right-hand margin to a stile on the right. Go over, turn left and follow the field margin. Cross a stile, pass **Wadfield Farm** and walk on a track to a road. Turn right. After 400yds (366m) turn left on to a steep path among trees. At a field turn left and follow its margin to the top. Go through a gate and turn left. Eventually go through another gate to arrive at **Belas Knap**.

This barrow, or communal grave, dating to approximately 2500 BC, has a 'false' portal (apparently to warn off intruders) of breathtakingly exact dry-stone work. The real entrances to the burial chambers are at the sides. The tomb is constructed of slabs of limestone, covered in turf. Just who precisely was entombed here is unknown but it is surmised that ancestor worship was widely practised and that the mound was opened many times over the centuries to admit further generations of worthy souls. No doubt the whole community worked at its construction over many months and maintained it devotedly. It is possible that the barrow became the centrepiece of the settlement. In all, 38 skeletons have been found inside the tomb.

Leave the **barrow** on the opposite side and walk ahead until you come to a track. Turn right and descend for about ½ mile (800m) to a road at a sharp corner, Point Ⓑ. Go left over a stile into a field and descend half right to another stile at the bottom. Turn right along a track. When you come to a road turn left and, after 500yds (457m), go right, through a kissing gate, into a field. Turn left and follow the margin until you come to a kissing gate and footbridge. Beyond, go up a path to the road. Turn right and make your way back to **Abbey Terrace**.

Whittington, Sevenhampton and Brockhampton

What happened when the Black Death came to Gloucestershire.

•DISTANCE•	7¼ miles (11.7km)
•MINIMUM TIME•	3hrs 30min
•ASCENT / GRADIENT•	280ft (85m) ▲▲ ▲
•LEVEL OF DIFFICULTY•	🚶🚶 🚶🚶 🚶
•PATHS•	Fields and tracks, 11 stiles
•LANDSCAPE•	Woodland, wolds, villages and distant views
•SUGGESTED MAP•	aqua3 OS Outdoor Leisure 45 The Cotswolds
•START / FINISH•	Grid reference: SP 010235
•DOG FRIENDLINESS•	On leads only occasionally, in fields with livestock
•PARKING•	Parking area at end of lane at Whitehall, on Cleeve Hill north west of Brockhampton
•PUBLIC TOILETS•	None on route

Walk 30 Directions

From the parking area walk along the lane towards **Brockhampton**. Just after a junction on your left turn right on to a footpath alongside a field. Cross a stile and continue on the same line across more stiles, following the path as it descends through undergrowth. Cross a field at the bottom to another stile and enter a large field.

Go forward, curving very gently left, passing through scrubland (where you might see the occasional waymarker). Eventually you will come to a fence on the left. Follow this and, at the point where telegraph poles on the right converge with the path, reach a stile on the left. Go over this on to a broad track. Follow it until you emerge in a large field. Cross the field, curving slightly left, to a gate. Go through, follow the track to the bottom and bear right to a road.

Turn left and, at a junction, turn right until you reach **Whittington Court**. The house is mainly Tudor but there has been a manor house on this site since well before the Normans – a moated version is mentioned in the Domesday Book. Earlier stonework is still visible at the base of the walls. The Church of St Bartholomew stands adjacent to the house. It may well be closed, but if it is open it is well worth the effort. You'll see the handsome brasses of Richard Coton – who built the present house – and his wife Margaret, as well as three Cotswold-stone effigies. Two are of

WHAT TO LOOK FOR

After passing Syreford Mill, and at the junction with the lane, look down to your left, where you will see a large old **mill stone**, presumably left over from a time when the mill was working. As you leave Brockhampton, you will see **Brockhampton House**, a largely 19th-century pile that has been converted into flats.

Richard de Crupes and his son, Richard, 13th-century lords of the manor, whilst the third is presumed to be the wife of one of them. It is said that the oak panelling in the chancel was made from the old pews of Sevenhampton church.

Walk 30

WHERE TO EAT AND DRINK

In Brockhampton, the **Craven Arms**, passed near the walk's end, serves a good restaurant-style lunch. The pub stands next to a high chimney, which is all that remains of Brockhampton's old village brewery.

A little way back up the road towards the village, look for a gate on the right into a field. Take the middle path by bearing slightly right to pass a spinney, continuing on the same line over some grassy bumps to a stile on the far side.

The grassy bumps are all that remain of Old Whittington. Although the plague – the 14th-century Black Death – devastated towns far more than rural areas, a good quarter of Gloucestershire's population was lost to it. Many villages were abandoned and then resettled near by – Whittington is a good example.

Now follow the left margin of a succession of fields more or less on the same line. The path then crosses a field's middle line to a stile. It then descends into a thicket beside a lake. Keep right of this, then follow a clear path left of **Syreford Mill** to a track. Turn left and continue until you come to a lane. Cross the road to a track. Follow this as it passes houses and curves right into woodland. Walk through the woods to emerge at the edge of a field. Cross this, enter another field and continue across to a gate.

Go through and follow the left side of a field to a gate on your left. Go through and follow a track down to a road. Turn left. Just before the ford at the **River Coln** turn right on to a grassy path. Follow this to a stile and a bridge. The path then climbs up a bank to a stile. Cross a field to a road and then enter **Sevenhampton churchyard**.

Sevenhampton was originally known as Sennington. The village was located on the opposite hill until the plague's onslaught. The parish church was embellished through the wealth of John Camber, a 15th-century wool merchant. Although small, its flying buttresses and impressive vaulting aspire to something greater. Overlooking the church is Sevenhampton Manor, built in 1550 and partially demolished in the 1950s.

Walk to the right of the **church** and then turn right into a newer burial area. Turn left to pass through a kissing gate into another field. Continue down beside a wall and enter the next field. Now go half right across the field to a kissing gate and follow a grassy path up into **Brockhampton**. Pass the former brewery, with its brick chimney, and then the **Craven Arms** pub, to a junction. Turn left up to a crossroads. Cross over and, at the next junction, turn right to return to the start.

WHILE YOU'RE THERE

Drive along the small lanes through the pretty countryside to the north and visit **Winchcombe** where you can visit Sudeley Castle or Belas Knap (► Walk 28/29). Alternatively visit the beautiful town of **Cheltenham** with its wide streets and acres of Georgian and Regency architecture.

A Ghostly Trail Around Prestbury

A gentle ramble around this unassuming old village which claims to be one of Britain's most haunted.

•DISTANCE•	3½ miles (5.7km)
•MINIMUM TIME•	1hr 30min
•ASCENT / GRADIENT•	100ft (30m) ▲ ▲ ▲
•LEVEL OF DIFFICULTY•	林 林 林
•PATHS•	Fields (could be muddy in places) and pavement, 10 stiles
•LANDSCAPE•	Woodland, hills and villages
•SUGGESTED MAP•	aqua3 OS Explorer 179 Gloucester, Cheltenham & Stroud
•START / FINISH•	Grid reference: SO 972238
•DOG FRIENDLINESS•	Lead necessary as some fields stocked with farm animals; some stiles have dog slots
•PARKING•	Free car park near war memorial
•PUBLIC TOILETS•	None on route

BACKGROUND TO THE WALK

The village of Prestbury, on the north east fringe of Cheltenham, is reputedly the second most haunted village in England, with The Burgage its oldest and most haunted street. The largest building along it is Prestbury House, now a hotel. During the Civil War it was occupied by Parliamentary troops. Expecting Royalists camped on Cleeve Hill to send a messenger to Gloucester, they laid a trap. A rope was stretched across The Burgage. When the galloping Cavalier rode through the village, he snagged on the rope and was catapulted from his mount. No doubt relieved of his despatches and interrogated, the unfortunate rider was then executed. A skeleton discovered near by in the 19th century is thought to be his. It is said that the sound of galloping hooves can often be heard here, as well as a horse's snorting and stamping.

Exercise and Exorcism

More paranormal activity has been experienced in the hotel grounds, where they meet Mill Street. Here there have been sightings of rowdy parties of people in Regency dress. On this site, it turns out, there was once a fashionable meeting place, called the Grotto. It was where the local gentry would take their ease. By the time of its closure, in 1859, it had become known as a place of ill-repute.

Spectral abbots are regularly seen in Prestbury. The Black Abbot used to walk the aisle of St Mary's Church but, since his exorcism, he prefers the churchyard – a vicar came across him here, seated on a tombstone. The Abbot has also been spotted in the early morning near the Plough Inn on Mill Street. In fact, there have been sightings of the Black Abbot almost everywhere in the village. Perhaps this may be explained by the fact that the Bishops of Hereford owned a palace here from the 12th century, whilst the Prior of Llanthony lived in the priory close to the church. There are severals other haunted places you will come across in the village. At Sundial Cottage, in The Burgage, a lovelorn girl plays the spinet; the Three

Queens house in Deep Street had to be exorcised; there are three stone cottages next to Three Queens, the middle one of which is haunted by soldiers from the Civil War, and the third of which is haunted by the Black Abbot. And another abbot (or perhaps the same one) with 'an unpleasant leer', is said to haunt Morningside House, next to the car park.

There is more to the village than ghosts, however. The manor of Prestbury, belonging to the Bishop of Hereford, was established by AD 899. Remains of the moated hall can still be found on Spring Lane, close to Cheltenham racecourse. By the 13th century Prestbury had gained a charter to hold a weekly market in The Burgage. This was also the site of the annual fair. The village is closely associated with the jockey Fred Archer, as a plaque on the King's Arms testifies, whilst the cricketer Charlie Parker, who played for England, was also born here. Another great English cricketer, Tom Graveney, was once landlord of the Royal Oak on The Burgage.

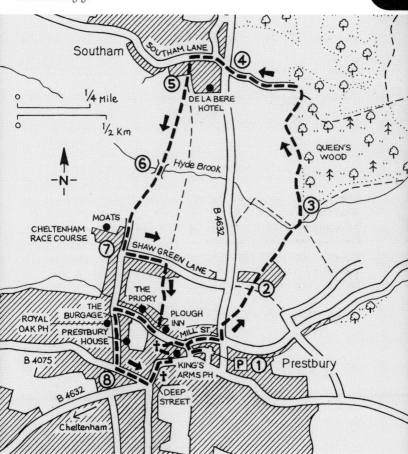

Walk 31 Directions

① Leave the car park, turn right into **The Bank** and right again into **Mill Street**. At the main road turn left. After 100yds (91m) cross the road to a stile. Go into a field and go diagonally left to another stile.

② Cross this and follow the track that is ahead of you and slightly to

Walk 31

your left. Where it goes right, cross a stile in front of you. Cross a field heading slightly to the right, to another stile. Go over this into a field and head for **Queen's Wood** in front of you.

③ Stay to the left of the woods. Eventually cross a track and enter another field. Where the woods sweep uphill, continue straight on through bushes to a bridle gate. Go through on to a woodland path and turn left, downhill, to reach the main road.

④ Ahead of you are the medieval buildings of the **De La Bere Hotel**. Cross the road and turn right. Follow the pavement as it bears left into **Southam Lane**. After 200yds (183m) turn left along a track to a gate. Go through this and a kissing gate to a field.

⑤ Head across, bearing slightly right, with the De La Bere on your left. Follow an obvious path across a series of paddocks and fields via stiles and gates. Finally, at a stile amid bushes in a corner, cross on to a track and follow this as it leads to a bridge stile.

⑥ Cross and continue straight ahead into a field with a hedge on your right. Go over the brow of the slope and down to a gate in the hedge to your right. Go through to a track and follow this to a road.

⑦ Turn left along **Shaw Green Lane**. After about 400yds (366m) turn right along a footpath passing between houses. Eventually this will bring you out on to **Mill Street**, opposite the church. Turn right, to walk past the **Priory** and the brick wall that marks the site of the haunted Grotto, until you come to **The Burgage**. Turn left here, passing the **Royal Oak**, **Prestbury House** and **Sundial Cottage**.

⑧ At the junction with **Tatchley Lane** turn left and then left again into **Deep Street**, passing the **Three Queens** and the trio of stone cottages. Just before the **Kings Arms** turn left on a footpath leading to the **church**. Turn right just before the church and pass through the churchyard to return to **Mill Street**, opposite the **Plough Inn**. Turn right and return to the car park at the start.

The Medieval Looters of Brimpsfield

A walk through a vanished castle and secluded valleys, taking in charming Syde and tiny Caudle Green.

•DISTANCE•	4 miles (6.4km)
•MINIMUM TIME•	2hrs
•ASCENT / GRADIENT•	180ft (55m) ▲▲ ▲ ▲
•LEVEL OF DIFFICULTY•	🚶 🚶 🚶
•PATHS•	Fields, tracks and pavement, 9 stiles
•LANDSCAPE•	Woodland, steep, narrow valleys and villages
•SUGGESTED MAP•	aqua3 OS Explorer 179 Gloucester, Cheltenham & Stroud
•START / FINISH•	Grid reference: SO 938124
•DOG FRIENDLINESS•	Some good, long stretches free of livestock
•PARKING•	Brimpsfield village; lay-bys on Cranham road
•PUBLIC TOILETS•	None on route

BACKGROUND TO THE WALK

There is something poignant about a vanished castle. The manor of Brimpsfield was given by William the Conqueror to the Giffard family. In early Norman French a 'gifard' was a person with fat cheeks and a double chin. The Giffards built two castles, the first of wood on another site, and its successor of stone, near Brimpsfield church. In 1322 John Giffard fell foul of King Edward II, following a rebellion that was quelled at the Battle of Boroughbridge in Yorkshire – Giffard was hanged at Gloucester.

Plundering Populace

Consequently the family castle was 'slighted', that is to say, put beyond all possible military use. In such circumstances local people were never slow to remove what was left for their own, non-military use. Now almost nothing remains of the castle apart from the empty meadow just before the church and some earthworks to its right. Some of the castle masonry found its way into the fabric of the church. On the stone shed to the left of the church there are details that appear to be medieval and which perhaps originally decorated the castle. The other possibility is that they formed part of a 12th-century priory, long since disappeared, that belonged to the abbey of Fontenay in Burgundy. Brimpsfield church, rather lonely without its castle, distinguishes itself on two counts. Several medieval tombstones, thought to commemorate members of the Giffard family, have been brought inside from the churchyard for their protection. The other, highly unusual feature, is the huge base of the tower, which separates the nave from the chancel. It is not clear how this came about, but it is surmised that the east wall would originally have contained an arch over which a bell turret was built in the 13th century, requiring the addition of more masonry. When the turret was replaced by a 15th-century tower still more masonry was needed to keep it upright.

The small and charming village of Syde overlooks the Frome Valley. Perched on the valley slope, the early Norman church in Syde has a saddleback tower and a rustic,

15th-century roof. It is worth peering inside to search out the 15th-century octagonal font and the small round window featuring St James, dating from the same period. The box pews are from the 17th century. Don't miss the ancient tithe barn just to the south of the church. Caudle Green is a typical example of a hamlet that has grown up around a single farm and expanded only very slightly over the centuries. It is dominated by an elegant, 18th-century farmhouse overlooking the village green.

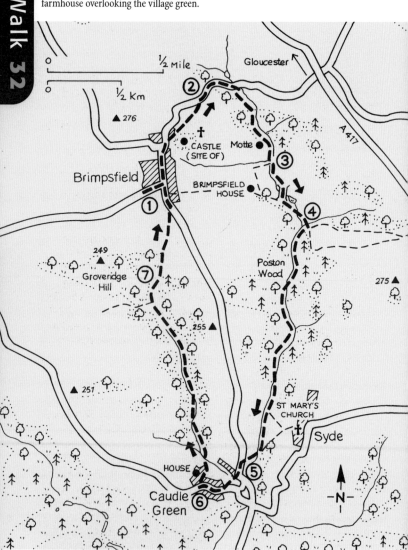

Walk 32 Directions

① Go to the end of the road towards the village centre and turn left. Walk through the village and, at the corner, turn right through a gate on to a track towards the **church**. Before the church bear left across the meadow (the site of the castle) to a stile. In the next field go half right to a corner and a road.

② Turn right and follow the road down to just before a cottage near the bottom. Turn right here on to a drive. After a few paces drop down to the left on to a parallel path which will bring you back on to the drive. Next, just before a cottage, turn left and go down into woodland to follow a path with the stream on your left. Follow this for 550yds (503m), ignoring a bridge on your left, to cross two stiles and emerge on to a track.

WHILE YOU'RE THERE

In nearby Miserden the Elizabethan mansion, **Misarden Park**, is set in pretty gardens; they are open on certain days throughout the summer months. Sir Edward Lutyens designed the war memorial here. Further west is **Whiteway**, where a group of libertarians from Essex established a proto-anarchist community, based on the ideas of Leo Tolstoy, in 1898.

③ Turn left and follow the track as it rises to the right. After 100yds (91m) go forward over a stile into a field with **Brimpsfield House** to your right. Go half right to another stile, pass a gate on your right and cross another stile at the next corner. Follow the path to cross a bridge and bear left up to a track. Follow this for 250yds (229m), until you come to a crossways.

④ Turn right to follow a footpath along the bottom of a valley. After ¾ mile (1.2km) the track will become grassy. Where houses appear above you to the left you can go left up the slope to visit the church at Syde. Otherwise remain on the valley floor and continue

WHERE TO EAT AND DRINK

There is nowhere on the route where refreshment is available, unless you make a diversion to the **Golden Hart** at Nettleton Bottom, (on the road to Cirencester). Otherwise you can seek out the **Carpenter's Arms** in Miserden to the south, or the **Black Horse** in Cranham to the west.

until you come to some gates. Take the one furthest to the right and go ahead to pass to the left of a cottage. Follow a drive up to a road.

⑤ Turn left and follow the road as it turns sharp left. At this point turn right over a stile into a field and walk up a steep bank to arrive in **Caudle Green**.

⑥ Turn right. At the green, just before a large house ahead of you, bear right to a stile and follow a winding path down to the valley bottom. Turn left, through a bridle gate, and follow the path along the valley bottom on the same line for ¾ mile (1.2km) until you come to a stile at a field.

⑦ Once you are in the field, continue up the slope until you come to a gate at a road. Turn left to re-enter **Brimpsfield**.

WHAT TO LOOK FOR

The little stream encountered at certain points during the walk is the infant **River Frome**, which, in its later, stronger stages to the south, runs through the Stroud Valley. The Frome powered the dozens of weaving mills that existed until the latter part of the 19th century. As you ascend the valley slope into Syde look out for the old **sheep dip** just below the village.

Sapperton, Daneway and the Thames & Severn Canal

Sapperton, both the focus of a major engineering project and a cradle for cultural change.

•DISTANCE•	6 miles (9.7km)
•MINIMUM TIME•	3hrs
•ASCENT / GRADIENT•	345ft (105m) ▲▲ ▲▲ ▲
•LEVEL OF DIFFICULTY•	🚶🚶 🚶🚶 🚶🚶
•PATHS•	Woodland paths and tracks, fields, lanes and canalside paths, 12 stiles
•LANDSCAPE•	Secluded valleys and villages
•SUGGESTED MAP•	aqua3 OS Explorer 168 Stroud, Tetbury and Malmesbury
•START / FINISH•	Grid reference: SO 948033
•DOG FRIENDLINESS•	Good – very few livestock
•PARKING•	In Sapperton village near church
•PUBLIC TOILETS•	None on route

BACKGROUND TO THE WALK

Sapperton was at the centre of two conflicting tendencies during the late 18th and early 20th centuries – the Industrial Revolution and the Romantic Revival. In the first case, it was canal technology that came to Sapperton. Canal construction was widespread throughout England from the mid-18th century onwards. Just as 'dot com' companies attracted vast sums of money in the late 1990s, so investors poured their money into 18th-century joint stock companies, regardless of their profitability. Confidence was high and investors expected to reap the rewards of commercial success based on the need to ship goods swiftly across the country.

Tunnel Vision

One key project was thought to be the canal that would link the River Severn and the River Thames. The main obstacle was the need for a tunnel through the Cotswolds, the cost of which could be unpredictable. But these were heady days and investors' money was forthcoming to press ahead with the scheme in 1783. During the tunnel's construction, the diarist and traveller John Byng visited the workings. With obvious distaste he wrote, 'I was enveloped in thick smoke arising from the gunpowder of the miners, at whom, after passing by many labourers who work by small candles, I did at last arrive; they come from the Derbyshire and Cornish mines, are in eternal danger and frequently perish by falls of earth'.

The Thames and Severn Canal opened in 1789, linking the Thames at Lechlade with the Stroudwater Navigation at Stroud. The Sapperton Tunnel, at 3,400yds (3,109m) long, is still one of the longest transport tunnels in the country. Barges were propelled through the tunnel by means of 'leggers', who 'walked' against the tunnel walls and who patronised the inns that are at both tunnel entrances. Yet the canal was not a success: either there was too much or too little water; rock falls and leakages required constant attention. The cost of maintaining the tunnel led to the closure of the canal in 1911.

The Arts and Crafts Movement

It isn't just the tunnel that is of interest in Sapperton. Some of the cottages here were built by disciples of William Morris (1834–96). He was the doyen of the Arts and Crafts Movement. It aspired to reintroduce to English life a simple yet decorative functionality, a reaction to the growing mass-production methods engendered by the Industrial Revolution. Furniture makers and architects like Ernest Gimson (from Leicestershire), Sidney and Ernest Barnsley (from Birmingham), and Norman Jewson all worked in Daneway, at Daneway House. Gimson and the Barnsley brothers are buried at Sapperton church. The finest example of their vernacular-style architecture in Sapperton is Upper Dorval House. The entrance to the western end of the Sapperton Tunnel is in fact in the hamlet of Daneway, a short walk along the path from the Daneway Inn, formerly called the Bricklayer's Arms. Daneway House, the 14th-century house that was let to followers of William Morris by Earl Bathurst, is a short distance up the road from the pub.

Walk 33 Directions

Walk 33

① With the church to your left, walk along a 'No Through Road'. This descends rapidly and, at the entrance to a house at the bottom, turn left on to a footpath.

② Continue uphill into **woodland**. Take the main path, ignoring a footpath on the left, but where it then forks, go left uphill. Climb to a junction of tracks. Turn left and stay on the track for ½ mile (800m) to a gate at a lane.

③ Turn left and then immediately right over a stile (opposite **Daneway House**). Take the first left and walk along a wide grassy area, with a fence to the right, to a stile at a lane. Turn right for 250yds (229m) then turn left over a stile.

> **WHILE YOU'RE THERE**
> Cirencester is not far away. As well as the **Corinium Museum** and the largest **parish church** in England, you can explore **Cirencester Park**. This fine estate was partly designed by the poet Alexander Pope for Lord Bathurst. and can be entered from Sapperton.

④ Walk down a drive. Just before the house go left through a hedge and turn immediately right, following a path to a stile. Cross this, then a bridge and a field, and a stile into woodland. Follow a path to a gate at a field, which you cross half right. Pass through a gate and head left of **Oakridge Farm** to another gate on to a lane.

⑤ Turn left and pass a junction. At a sharp right corner go ahead into a field. Walk to a stile on the far side. Cross the next field and find a stile in the top right corner (Point Ⓐ on Walk 34). Follow the left margin of the next field to a road. Turn left along the road through **Oakridge**.

⑥ At a crossroads turn right, climbing to a road. Turn left (Point Ⓑ). At the **green** go to the end and bear right to a stile. Enter a field, keep close to a hedge on the left and cross two further stiles. Bear right across a field to a stile into woodland. Descend steeply and turn left on to a path, which you follow to a junction. Turn left down to a road.

> **WHERE TO EAT AND DRINK** ⓘ
> On this walk you are very well provided for – there is a pub in every village you walk through. In Sapperton the **Bell**, near the church, is worth a visit. In Oakridge the **Butcher's Arms** requires only a short diversion. In Daneway the **Daneway Inn** is on your route.

⑦ Turn left then, at a junction, turn right to cross a bridge. Bear left and, a few paces after, turn left again over a footbridge then right on to a footpath. Follow the canal for 600yds (549m). Cross a bridge and turn left on a path to a road by the **Daneway Inn**. Turn right and then left to continue by the canal to the **Sapperton Tunnel**. Walk above the tunnel's portico to a field. Bear half right up to a stile. Cross to a path and walk up to a lane which leads back into **Sapperton**.

> **WHAT TO LOOK FOR** ⓘ
> Emerging on the road after Oakridge Farm you are at the edge of the hamlet of **Far Oakridge**. Painter William Rothenstein lived at Iles Farm between 1913 and 1920, hosting the poets W H Davies and Rabindranath Tagore. Writer and caricaturist Max Beerbohm resided at nearby Winstons Cottage, as did, later, the poet John Drinkwater.

Queen Elizabeth I and the Bisley Boy

Take this extension, which makes for a much longer walk, to visit Bisley, one of the Cotswolds loveliest villages.
See map and information panel for Walk 33

•DISTANCE•	10 miles (16.1km)
•MINIMUM TIME•	4hrs 30min
•ASCENT / GRADIENT•	1,165ft (355m) ▲▲▲
•LEVEL OF DIFFICULTY•	🚶🚶🚶

Walk 34 Directions (Walk 33 option)

From Point Ⓐ go half right to a stile. Turn left along a track to a road and turn right. After ½ mile (800m), at a crossroads at **Far Oakridge**, turn left on to a track. Where this track ends continue to a junction at **Waterlane**. Take the left-hand lane opposite. At a junction at a farm turn left, following this track to a gate at a **spinney**.

Proceed into, and cross, a field to a stile at some **woodland**. Follow a steep path down to a stile. Descend a field, turning left before the bottom. Walk through fields, crossing stiles and then bear right up to a track. Turn left and walk all the way to a junction. Turn right along a track and enter a field. Go half left to the other side and left along a path to a road. Cross this carefully, watching for traffic, and descend some steps into the middle of **Bisley** village.

In Bisley, legend says, the real Queen Elizabeth I is buried. Apparently, during a visit here as a young girl, she fell ill and died. A local boy who closely resembled her took her place and went on to become queen…

Turn left and take the first left up a street to a junction. Enter the road opposite, follow it as it goes sharp right. After 400yds (366m), opposite **Rectory Farm**, turn right through a gate and continue to a road. Cross to a stile and then a paddock to another stile. Go half right across two fields and then half right to a gap and then another. Turn left to a stile in the corner and head for a stile at the edge of trees. Go down a path to a small field. Go half right to cross a track and a stile. Cross to a path alongside houses and descend left into **Bournes Green**.

Turn right to a junction, then turn left. At the next junction descend a grassy bank and turn left. Follow the road down and up again to a corner. Turn right over a stile, then half left up a bank of trees to another stile. Continue across fields to a road and turn right. At the next junction turn right, passing a road on the left (Point Ⓑ). Continue to Point ⑥ on Walk 33.

Turbulent Tewkesbury

Tracing the military movements that culminated in the Battle of Tewkesbury.

•**DISTANCE**•	4¼ miles (6.8km)
•**MINIMUM TIME**•	2hrs
•**ASCENT / GRADIENT**•	35ft (10m)
•**LEVEL OF DIFFICULTY**•	
•**PATHS**•	Fields, pavement and lanes, 4 stiles
•**LANDSCAPE**•	River, distant hills and town
•**SUGGESTED MAP**•	aqua3 OS Explorer 190 Malvern Hills & Bredon Hill
•**START / FINISH**•	Grid reference: SO 891325
•**DOG FRIENDLINESS**•	Traffic on main roads so on lead – otherwise quite good
•**PARKING**•	Street parking and parks, most convenient on Gander Lane
•**PUBLIC TOILETS**•	On main road near Tewkesbury Abbey

Walk 35 Directions

The walk begins at **Gander Lane**, north east of **Tewkesbury Abbey**.

This spectacular Norman construction dominates the town, which is situated at the confluence of the Rivers Severn and Avon. It was partly this geography which made Tewkesbury the site of one of the most important battles in English history.

Walk away from the town centre. Cross the **River Swilgate** and continue to a pair of iron gates. Stay on the path as it traverses the area known as the Vineyards, where the monks of the abbey once cultivated grapes. Pass a commemorative

WHAT TO LOOK FOR ⓘ

As you walk around the town, look out for the **narrow alleys** – with their entertaining names – that lead off Tewkesbury's main streets. They owe their existence to the tendency for the Severn to flood, forcing the population to make the best use of available space.

plinth on your right and keep to the left of the **cemetery**. It was along here that a Lancastrian army, consisting of over 6,000 men, stood on 4th May 1471, facing towards the south.

The conflict between the Houses of York and Lancaster had already lasted for 20 years. The Yorkist Edward IV was in exile and the Lancastrian Henry VI had been restored to the throne through the machinations of the Earl of Warwick. In April 1471 Edward returned to England, defeated Warwick and imprisoned Henry. Margaret of Anjou, Henry's consort, headed for Wales to drum up further support, but at Tewkesbury, a crossing point of the Severn, her army was intercepted by Edward.

Continue along the path as it passes close to the cemetery and you will soon arrive at a road. Cross the road and turn right towards a house, taking the path that runs along its left flank. This will bring you on to **Gloucester Road**, at a point where a wing of the Yorkist

> **WHERE TO EAT AND DRINK** ⓘ
> Tewkesbury has a wide range of pubs and restaurants to choose from. Some have historical or literary associations. **Gupshill Manor** has connections with the Battle of Tewkesbury, whilst the **Royal Hop Pole** is where Mr Pickwick feasted in Dickens' *The Pickwick Papers*.

army stood. Turn left along the pavement. Shortly after a bus stop turn left along a path, towards houses. At the end turn right to follow another path, turning left at a corner. This brings you to a gate on your right which leads into the field known as **Margaret's Camp**. The field is so-called after Margaret of Anjou, as it is traditionally thought to be the place where the Lancastrian army bivouacked on the eve of the battle.

Cross the field to a gate on the far side, emerging on to a road beside houses. Turn right, return to Gloucester Road and turn right again, passing **Gupshill Manor** across the road. Now a restaurant, Gupshill Manor is where Queen Margaret is said to have stayed the night before the battle. Continue towards the centre of **Tewkesbury** and, after about 800yds (732m), cross the road to a stile beside a bus stop to enter a field. Walk to the other side and in the corner cross another stile. This is thought to be the point where King Edward stood. Continue ahead between a barn and a house to reach a lane. In the field before you stood the wing of the Yorkist army led by Edward's brother, the Duke of Gloucester, later Richard III.

Turn right and continue to a junction, close to where the first clash of the battle occurred. Margaret's army suffered a bloody

defeat at the hands of Edward and the Yorkist cause remained safe for 14 years, until the Battle of Bosworth in 1485. Turn right and after about 50yds (46m) turn left through a kissing gate into **Bloody Meadow**, where the remnants of the Lancastrian right wing were slain. Pass through bushes to a stile and then on to a road. Turn right and continue to meet **Gloucester Road** yet again. Opposite are the Vineyards, into which the demoralised Lancastrians fled, some taking refuge in the abbey. After two days they were given up, only to face execution in the abbey grounds. Altogether 2,000 Lancastrians were killed.

> **WHILE YOU'RE THERE** ⓘ
> The **John Moore Museum** on Church Street is an interesting countryside museum commemorating the local author, John Moore. His books, all set in the first part of the 20th century, depict everyday life in Tewkesbury and the surrounding countryside.

Turn left and follow the pavement until you come to the **Bell** at the corner of **Mill Street**. Turn left here, down to the **Abbey Mill**, which featured in Dinah Craik's *John Halifax, Gentleman* (1857). Now cross on to **The Ham**. Turn right to follow the bank of the **Mill Avon** towards a large flour mill. Just before it, turn right over a footbridge across the Mill Avon, bringing you on to **Tolsey Lane**. Turn left and follow this as it curves right to bring you to the **High Street** with its famous timber-framed houses. Turn right here and walk the length of the street, back to the junction with **Barton Street** and **Church Street**. Keep right to enter Church Street and then turn left back into **Gander Lane**.

Painswick's Traditions

From the Queen of the Cotswolds through the Washpool Valley.

•DISTANCE•	7½ miles (12.1km)
•MINIMUM TIME•	3hrs 30min
•ASCENT / GRADIENT•	705ft (215m) ▲▲▲
•LEVEL OF DIFFICULTY•	🚶🚶 🚶🚶 🚶
•PATHS•	Fields, tracks, golf course and a green lane, 16 stiles
•LANDSCAPE•	Hills, valleys, villages, isolated farmhouses, extensive views
•SUGGESTED MAP•	aqua3 OS Explorer 179 Gloucester, Cheltenham & Stroud
•START / FINISH•	Grid reference: SO 865094
•DOG FRIENDLINESS•	Off leads along lengthy stretches, many stiles
•PARKING•	Car park (small fee) near library, just off main road
•PUBLIC TOILETS•	At car park

BACKGROUND TO THE WALK

Local traditions continue to thrive in Painswick, the 'Queen of the Cotswolds'. These are centred around its well-known churchyard, where the Victorian poet Sydney Dobell is buried. The churchyard is famously filled, not only with the 'table' tombs of 18th-century clothiers, but also with 99 beautifully manicured yew trees, planted in 1792. The legend goes that only 99 will ever grow at any one time, as Old Nick will always kill off the hundredth. Should you be minded to do so, try to count them. You will almost certainly be thwarted, as many of them have grown together, creating arches and hedges.

This old tale has become confused with an ancient ceremony that still takes place here on the Sunday nearest to the Feast of the Nativity of St Mary, in mid-September. This is the 'clipping' ceremony, which has absolutely nothing to do with cutting bushes or flowers. It derives from the old Saxon word, 'clyping', which means 'embrace' and is used in conjunction with the church. Traditionally, the children of the village gather together on the Sunday afternoon and join hands to form a circle around the church or churchyard, and advance and retreat to and from the church, singing the *Clipping Hymn*. Perhaps this ceremony is the distant descendant of an age-old pagan ceremony involving a ritual dance around an altar bearing a sacrificed animal. The children wear flowers in their hair and are rewarded with a coin and a bun for their efforts. There was, and maybe still is, a special cake baked for the day, known as 'puppy dog pie', in which a small china dog was inserted. Was this a reminder of the ancient ritual sacrifice? There are yew trees in other gardens in the village, many of them older than those in the churchyard, and one of which is said to have been planted by Queen Elizabeth I.

The other famous tradition that continues to be observed in the area takes place further along the escarpment, at Cooper's Hill. Here, on Spring Bank Holiday Monday, the cheese-rolling races take place. From a spot marked by a maypole, competitors hurtle down an absurdly steep slope in pursuit of wooden discs representing Gloucester cheeses. The winner, or survivor, is presented with a real cheese; but the injury rate is high and there has been a lot of controversy about whether the event should be allowed to continue. Fortunately, tradition has won the day so far and people are still able to break their necks in the pursuit of cheese if they want to.

Walk 36

239 ▲

½ Mile

½ km

-N-

③ Painswick Hill
283 ▲ TRIG POINT Fort
SPOONBED FARM
A 46
UPPER HOLCOMBE FARM
Cheltenham
④
HOLCOMBE HOUSE
B 4073
241 ▲ GOLF COURSE
HOLCOMBE FARM
⑤
② CEMETERY
205 ▲
EDGE FARM
A 4173
Wash Brook
PAINSWICK HOUSE AND ROCOCO GARDENS
A 46
Edge
⑥
EDGE HILL FARM
WC P ①
PAINSWICK
EDGEMOOR INN
▲ 225
Scottsquar Hill
A 4173
KING'S MILL
⑦
Painswick stream
SHEEPHOUSE
Pitchcombe
A 46
PINCOT LANE
Juniper Hill ▲ 232
↙ Stroud
PRIMROSE COTTAGE
Slad

Walk 36

Walk 36 Directions

① Turn right out of the car park and along the main street. Turn left along the **Gloucester road**, join another road and turn right towards the golf club. Bear left through the car park, turn left along a track and immediately right across a fairway (look out for flying golf balls).

> **WHAT TO LOOK FOR** ⓘ
> Just before you leave the golf course, at the highest point of the walk, you should be able to identify the ramparts and ditches of a **hill fort** beneath your feet. Like many such features on the Cotswold escarpment, this one is believed to date back to the Iron Age.

② Keep to the left of a **cemetery**, then cross another fairway to a woodland path. Continue to a road. After a few paces turn right. Walk along the edge of the golf course to the top of a promontory, passing to the left of a **trig point**. Descend the other side and turn left down a path. At a track go left to a road.

③ Turn right to a bus stop. Cross to a path going right. Turn left down to **Spoonbed Farm**. Walk through to a gate, then take a path to a field. In a second field keep left of a tree to reach a stile. After another stile cross a field to the right of a telegraph pole. Keep to the right of **Upper Holcombe Farm** to a stile.

④ Turn left, eventually ascending to **Holcombe Farm**. Continue along a track, passing some gates on the left, and go left into the next field. Cross a stile and bear right to another stile. Turn right down to a bridge, then take the rightmost path. Ascend the field to a stile.

⑤ Turn left towards **Edge Farm**, then fork right to a gate. Cross two fields to another gate. Pass a house, soon arriving at a road. Keep right. Opposite a house turn left over a stile, bear half right to another stile and enter **Edge**.

⑥ Turn left, then sharp right. Before the farm turn left over a stile, then another, to a bridge. Ascend a field to a stile, then head for a gate at a track, to the right of a farm. Go through another gate opposite and turn left up to a gate. Turn left and, after a few paces, turn right on to a track. Cross fields on the same line, passing right of a house to a road.

> **WHERE TO EAT AND DRINK** ⓘ
> There are several possibilities in Painswick – a pub, a tea room, a couple of restaurants and several shops. There is also a pub in Edge, the **Edgemoor Inn**, (a few minutes walk off the route).

⑦ Turn left, cross the **A46** and walk along **Pincot Lane**. At **Primrose Cottage** turn left over a stile and then cross to another. Cross a bridge, a stile and a gate to the left of **Sheephouse**. Walk along the drive and, where it forks, go left down to **King's Mill**. Bear right over the weir and then continue on the same line to arrive at a lane. Turn left to return to the start.

> **WHILE YOU'RE THERE** ⓘ
> Just outside the village are the **Painswick Rococo Gardens**. Here an 18th-century house is set in gardens that have been restored to how they would have appeared at the time of the house's construction. The detail for this restoration came from a contemporary painting. The garden is particularly well-known for the masses of snowdrops that appear there in the winter.

Walking with Rosie in the Slad Valley

A stroll through the countryside around Slad, backcloth to Laurie Lee's most popular novel.

•DISTANCE•	4 miles (6.4km)
•MINIMUM TIME•	2hrs
•ASCENT / GRADIENT•	425ft (130m) ▲▲▲
•LEVEL OF DIFFICULTY•	🚶🚶 🚶 🚶
•PATHS•	Tracks, fields and quiet lanes, 13 stiles
•LANDSCAPE•	Hills, valleys and woodland
•SUGGESTED MAP•	aqua3 OS Explorer 179 Gloucester, Cheltenham & Stroud
•START / FINISH•	Grid reference: SO 878087
•DOG FRIENDLINESS•	Mostly off leads – livestock encountered occasionally
•PARKING•	Lay-by at Bull's Cross
•PUBLIC TOILETS•	None on route

BACKGROUND TO THE WALK

The Slad Valley is one of the least spoiled parts of the Cotswolds, notwithstanding its invariable association with the area's most important literary figure, the poet Laurie Lee (1914–97). And yet he is not instantly remembered for his poetry but for *Cider With Rosie* (1959). This autobiographical account of a Cotswold childhood has, for thousands of students, been part of their English Literature syllabus.

A Childhood Gone Forever

For anyone coming to the area, *Cider With Rosie* is well worth reading, but it is especially pertinent here as it is largely set in Slad, where Lee was brought up and lived for much of his life. The book charts, in poetic language, the experiences of a child living in a world that is within living memory and yet has quite disappeared. Some of the episodes recounted in the book are said to have been products of Lee's imagination but, as he said himself, it was the 'feeling' of his childhood that he was endeavouring to capture.

A Spanish Odyssey

The story of his life is, anyway, an interesting one. He spent a considerable time in Spain and became involved in the Spanish Civil War and the struggle against Franco. Afterwards he established a reputation as a poet, mixing with the literati of the day. He was never very prolific – much of his energy appears to have been poured into love affairs. He did, however, write plays for radio and was involved in film-making during the Second World War. But it was with the publication of *Cider With Rosie* that he became a household name. Readers from all over the world identified with his magical evocation of rural English life and the book has not been out of print since. To some extent Lee became a prisoner of a *Cider with Rosie* industry. The picture of an avuncular figure living a bucolic idyll was not a strictly accurate one – much of his time was spent in London. He was susceptible to illness all his life. Nonetheless, in his later years he managed to complete his autobiographical trilogy. His second volume, *As I Walked Out One Midsummer Morning* (1969) describes his journey from Gloucestershire to Spain as an itinerant fiddle player. The third, *A Moment of War* (1991), recounts his experiences there during the Civil War. Lee died in 1997 and is buried in Slad churchyard. Many of the places in and around the village mentioned in *Cider With Rosie* are readily identifiable today. Although it is no longer possible to frolic in the roads with impunity, the valley remains as beautiful as it ever was.

Walk 37 **Directions**

① From **Bull's Cross** walk to the end of the lay-by (going south) and turn left on to a tarmac-covered drive. Follow it down and, immediately before some buildings, turn left over a stile into a field. Go half right, down the field and up the other side, to a gate at the top. Turn left along a track. Where it joins another track stay right and continue to a lane.

② Turn right and walk to the bottom. Pass between a large pond and **Steanbridge Mill**. If you want to visit Slad, follow the lane into the village. To continue the walk turn left immediately after the pond and walk to a stile. Cross into a field, with a hedge on your right, and continue to a stile at the top.

③ Cross and follow a path to another stile. Cross the next field and another stile, then continue as the path curves right towards a farm. Pass through a gate on to a track, stay to the right of **Furners Farm** and curve left. About 30yds (27m) after the curve turn right over a stile on to a wooded path and then, after a few paces, go right again over a stile into a field. Walk ahead, with the farm above you to the right. Cross another stile and then keep to the right of a pond.

WHILE YOU'RE THERE ⓘ

In its heyday **Stroud** was the centre of the 19th-century wool weaving industry. The small town centre offers a pleasant stroll featuring the Shambles, the Town Hall and the Subscription Rooms. There are a couple of museums to enjoy, including the Stroud Museum and the Industrial Museum.

WHAT TO LOOK FOR ⓘ

There are a number of landmarks on or near the walk that are readily associated with *Cider With Rosie*, including **Steanbridge Mill**. From Folly Lane, a short distance south of where you join it, there are often excellent **views** across to the River Severn and its bridges.

---

④ At the top of the pond cross a stile into a field. Go half left across it to a gate and stile. In the next field head straight across its lower part. At a point where a telegraph pole almost meets a hedge, turn right over a stile on to a track. Turn left to meet a lane.

⑤ Turn right and follow the lane to the valley bottom. Start to climb the other side and at a corner go over a stile on your right. Ascend steeply to another stile at the road. Turn right along the pavement. After 150yds (137m) cross to a footpath and climb steeply. At a junction of paths bear left and continue to a field. Follow the margin of the field up, then follow the path as it weaves in and out of **woodland**.

⑥ At the top turn right on to **Folly Lane** and continue to a junction. If you want to go into Slad, turn right, otherwise continue ahead on to a path that will soon take you into woodland. Walk through the woods, finally emerging at your starting point at **Bull's Cross**.

WHERE TO EAT AND DRINK ⓘ

The **Woolpack** in Slad features in *Cider With Rosie*. Laurie Lee was a regular there in his later years. It has since become well-known for its food. In the neighbouring village of Sheepscombe is the **Butcher's Arms**.

Weaving Along the Stroud Valley

Discover the impact of the Industrial Revolution in the steep-sided Cotswold valleys.

•DISTANCE•	6 miles (9.7km)
•MINIMUM TIME•	3hrs
•ASCENT / GRADIENT•	495ft (150m) ▲▲▲
•LEVEL OF DIFFICULTY•	🚶🚶 🚶🚶 🚶
•PATHS•	Fields, lanes, canal path and tracks, 3 stiles
•LANDSCAPE•	Canal, road and railway, valley and steep slopes, villages
•SUGGESTED MAP•	aqua3 OS Explorer 168 Stroud, Tetbury and Malmesbury
•START / FINISH•	Grid reference: SO 892025
•DOG FRIENDLINESS•	Good, with few stiles and little livestock
•PARKING•	Lay-by east of Chalford church
•PUBLIC TOILETS•	None on route

BACKGROUND TO THE WALK

Wool has been associated with the Cotswolds for many centuries. During the Middle Ages the fleece of the 'Cotswold Lion' breed was the most prized in all of Europe. Merchants from many countries despatched their agents to purchase it from the fairs and markets of the wold towns in the northern part of the region – most famously Northleach, Cirencester and Chipping Campden. Woven cloth eventually became a more important export and so the industry moved to the southern Cotswolds, with its steeper valleys and faster-flowing streams, which were well suited to powering woollen mills.

Mechanisation

The concentration of mills in the Stroud area was evident by the early 15th century. Indeed, its importance was such that in a 1557 Act of Parliament that restricted cloth manufacture to towns, the villages of the Stroud area were exempted. By 1700 the lower Stroud Valley was producing 30,000 bolts (about 4.59 million sq m) of cloth every year. At this time the spinning and weaving was done in domestic dwellings or workhouses, the woven cloth then being returned to the mill for fulling, roughening and shearing. The mills were driven by the natural flow of the streams but the Industrial Revolution was to bring rapid change. There was great opposition to the introduction of mechanical spinning and shearing machines. This was heightened in 1795 by the development of the improved broadloom with its flying shuttle. The expectation was that, as well as compelling weavers to work in the mills rather that at home, it would bring mass unemployment. Progress marched on, however, and by the mid-19th century there were over 1,000 looms at work in the Stroud Valley. They came with their share of political unrest too, and in 1825 and 1828 strikes and riots had to be quelled by troops. The industry went into decline through the course of the 19th century, as steam replaced water power and it migrated northwards to the Pennines. By 1901 only 3,000 people were employed in the cloth industry, compared with 24,000 in the mid-17th century. Today, only one mill remains.

Graceful Elevations

This walk begins in Chalford, an attractive village built on the steep sides of the Stroud Valley. Its streets are lined with terraces of 18th- and 19th-century clothiers' houses and weavers' cottages. On the canalside the shells of woollen mills are still plentiful.

The 18th-century church contains fine examples of craftsmanship from the 'Arts and Crafts' period of the late 19th century. Nether Lypiatt Manor is a handsome manor house now owned by Prince and Princess Michael of Kent. Known locally as 'the haunted house', it was built in 1702 for Judge Charles Cox. Its classical features and estate railings, all unusual in the Cotswolds, inspired wealthy clothiers to spend their money on the addition of graceful elevations to their own houses.

Walk 38

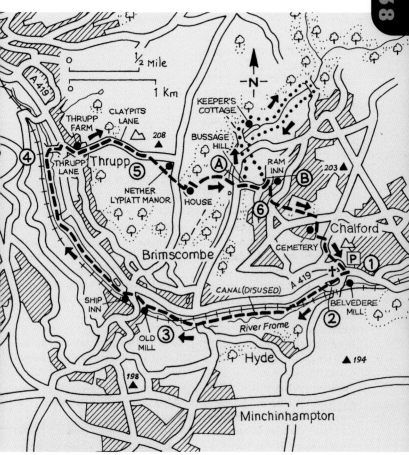

Walk 38 **Directions**

① Walk towards **Chalford church**. Immediately before it, cross the road and locate a path going right, towards a canal roundhouse. Note the **Belvedere Mill** across to your

left and follow the tow path alongside the **Thames and Severn Canal** on your right.

② Cross a road and continue along the tow path as it descends steps. Now follow this path for about 2 miles (3.2km). It will soon disappear under the railway line via a gloomy culvert, so that the **railway** will now be on your right, beyond the old canal. Old mills and small factories line the route.

③ Shortly before arriving in **Brimscombe** the path passes beneath the railway again. Soon after, it becomes a road leading into an industrial estate. At a road opposite a large, old mill turn left, to come to a junction. Cross and turn right. Immediately after the **Ship Inn** turn left along a road among offices and workshops. Continue straight on along a path, with factory walls to your right. The canal reappears on your left. As you walk on into the country you will pass beneath three brick bridges and a metal footbridge.

WHILE YOU'RE THERE ℹ️

High up on the far side of the Stroud Valley, there are a number of places to go. **Woodchester** has a well-preserved, Roman mosaic and an unfinished, 19th-century gothic mansion. **Rodborough Common** is the site of an 18th- and 19th-century fort that was originally built as a luxurious palace by a wealthy wool dyer. At **Selsley** is a little church filled with stained glass designed by members of the Arts and Crafts Movement.

---

④ At the next bridge, with a hamlet high on your left, turn right to follow a path to a road. Cross this and turn left. After a few paces turn right up a short path to meet **Thrupp Lane**. Turn right. At the top, turn left into **Claypits Lane**, turn right just before **Thrupp Farm** and climb up steeply.

WHAT TO LOOK FOR ℹ️

As you walk along the Stroudwater Canal look out for the **birds** that like to creep among the reeds: moorhens and coots, of course, but occasionally a heron will suddenly launch itself up from out of the undergrowth. Voles and stoats can be seen, and even the occasional adder.

---

⑤ After a long climb, as the road levels out, you will see **Nether Lypiatt Manor** in front of you. Turn right, beside a tree, over a stile into a field. Go half left to the far corner. Cross a stone stile and follow a narrow path beside trees to a road. Descend a lane opposite. Where it appears to fork, go straight on, to descend past a house. Enter **woodland** and fork right near the bottom. Keep a pond on your left and cross a road to climb **Bussage Hill**. After 100yds (91m) pass a lane on the left (Point Ⓐ on Walk 39). At the top fork left. Opposite the **Ram Inn** (Point Ⓑ) turn right.

⑥ After a telephone box and bus shelter turn left to follow a path among houses into woodland. Go ahead until you meet a road. Turn left and immediately right down a path beside a **cemetery**. Descend to another road. Turn right for 50yds (46m), then turn left down a steep lane among trees, leading back to **Chalford**. At the bottom turn left to return to the start of the walk.

WHERE TO EAT AND DRINK ℹ️

There are two easy possibilities en route: the **Ship Inn** at Brimscombe and the **Ram Inn** at Bussage. Only a short distance from Brimscombe is Stroud, which has several restaurants and cafes.

Spinning Off into the Toadsmoor Valley

Extend Walk 38 with a visit to this relatively inaccessible little valley.
See map and information panel for Walk 38

•DISTANCE•	8 miles (12.9km)
•MINIMUM TIME•	4hrs
•ASCENT / GRADIENT•	495ft (150m) ▲▲▲
•LEVEL OF DIFFICULTY•	👫 👫 👫

Walk 39 Directions (Walk 38 option)

The Cotswolds, for all their obvious charm, manage to conceal plenty of happy surprises. Many of these are only really accessible on foot – the **Toadsmoor Valley** is one.

From Point Ⓐ turn left along a track and follow it to a road. Cross this to a lane and follow this down, right, to a bridge and a ford.

This exquisite wooded valley runs between the Golden Valley at Brimscombe and a point just west of Bisley. In the past there were mills here, now long gone, although the weavers' cottages that preceded the mills remain. Cross and stay on the track as it bears right with a huge **pond** on your right.

This pond spreads along the valley bottom at the foot of a steep slope covered in tall trees. In the autumn these are a breathtaking sight. The pond is a haven for wildlife, including the grey heron, the largest of European herons. Follow this track for just under ¾ mile (1.2km), passing to the right of **Keeper's**

Cottage, until it rises to a country lane. (On the lake side of the track, opposite **Keeper's Cottage**, is a formal landscaped garden, something of a surprise in the midst of nature's exuberance.) Turn right to cross a bridge and then, opposite a house on the left, enter a track on the right. This will climb steadily and take you high above the valley below.

The steep, winding lanes that characterise this part of the Cotswolds were just wide enough to accept pack animals laden with spun or woven wool. Stay on this, passing through gates and crossing stiles where they arise, all the way to its end, bringing you to a road on the left.

Cross the road to steps leading up to a stone stile. Cross to **woodland** and follow a rising path which eventually leads to a stile. Go over into a field and straight ahead with a hedge on your right. At the top turn right and walk along the left side of a field to arrive at a stile at the edge of woodland. Cross over to a woodland path and follow it to a steep lane in **Bussage**. Turn left and climb up to a junction by the **Ram Inn**, Point Ⓑ.

Around Tetbury Town and Country

Walk 40

This handsome Cotswold town has kept its appeal without allowing conservation to leach it of its character.

•DISTANCE•	3½ miles (5.7km)
•MINIMUM TIME•	1hr 30min
•ASCENT / GRADIENT•	100ft (30m) ▲ ▲▲ ▲
•LEVEL OF DIFFICULTY•	👫 👫 👫
•PATHS•	Fields, lanes and tracks, 8 stiles
•LANDSCAPE•	Rolling hills, farmland and town
•SUGGESTED MAP•	aqua3 OS Explorer 168 Stroud, Tetbury & Malmesbury
•START / FINISH•	Grid reference: ST 890931
•DOG FRIENDLINESS•	On leads in town and in one section with animals
•PARKING•	Several car parks in central area near church
•PUBLIC TOILETS•	Old Brewery Lane or behind Snooty Fox on Chipping Lane

Walk 40 **Directions**

The centre of Tetbury is built around the Market Place, dominated by the pillared Market House. Built in 1655, it was later enlarged to accommodate the town's fire engine and lock-up. The Police Bygones Museum, on Long Street in the former Police Station, contains a collection of relics of Cotswold law enforcement in the old cells.

From the centre of the town pass the **Market Hall** on your right and then the **Snooty Fox Hotel**. Walk down **The Chipping** and then pass the **Priory** on your left. The road descends and passes the steep **Chipping Steps** on your right. 'Chipping' is an old English word for market. The area close to the steps, lined with weavers' cottages, was for centuries the site of 'Mop Fairs', where the unemployed could offer their services for domestic and

farming posts. Continue along the road, passing **Gumstool Hill** on the right. The hill is used for the annual woolsack races. There was once a ducking-stool or gum-stool here, used for the punishment of 'scolds'.

Tetbury's most attractive aspect is its streets of stone houses of all styles and of all ages. In the main they are used today as they always have been – as residences and places of work. Tetbury's early prosperity was based on the wool trade, but in the 18th century industrial demand for fast-flowing water, which Tetbury was unable to provide, led to the town's decline. As with other

> ### WHILE YOU'RE THERE
> Visit **Westonbirt Arboretum**, just over 3 miles (4.8km) to the south of Tetbury. It is one of the largest collections of trees and shrubs in the world. Although interesting to visit at any time of year, the autumn colours are truly resplendent because of the number of Japanese maples that flourish here.

towns and villages in the Cotswolds, this did have one happy consequence – Tetbury has not been blighted by inappropriate development. Unusually, however, its modern prosperity and vitality are not dependent exclusively on tourism. On the contrary, tourism here is the gilt on the gingerbread, which makes it a very pleasant place to visit.

WHERE TO EAT AND DRINK

On the square is the well-known **Snooty Fox**, a former coaching inn. (It was called the White Hart from the late 16th century until the 1960s.) During the 19th century it also acted as Assembly Rooms in an attempt to attract the cream of society. There are many other pubs and cafes scattered about the town.

Just before the **Royal Oak** turn right along a lane. Keeping to the left of a transformer station, follow this lane all the way to a gate at a field. Go through and walk straight ahead. Go to the top of a knoll and then descend on the other side, keeping to the right of a fence to cross a stream by a stone bridge. Continue along the path to a gate. Go through and then half left up a bank to another gate (ignoring a first gate on your left). Go through and then bear left to follow a path along a grassy area of shrubs. Follow this around to the right, pass a cottage on the left and a farm on the right and join a track. Stay on this and follow it all the way to a lane, where you turn right.

Stay on this for ⅔ mile (1.1km) and then, opposite a track on the left, turn right over a stile into a field. Walk along the field edge, skirting a pond, then carry on to find another stile, in the general direction of **Tetbury church**. The parish church

is in complete contrast with almost every other church in the Cotswolds. It is a striking example of late 18th-century Georgian Gothic. Its spire is one of the highest in the country and its interior is delicate and simple.

Go over the stile and cross the field to a gate. In the next field head for some farm buildings but, just before them, turn right through a gate into a farmyard. Turn left to walk through the farmyard and continue on to a track. Stay on this until, just before a large house, you find a stone stile in front of you. Go over it and turn right over a stile into a field. Turn immediately left and walk along the left side of the field, with houses on the left, all the way to the far corner.

Go down to a road and turn right along the pavement to a track on the left, just before a bridge. Follow this down until, after a stone bridge, you turn right up to a kissing gate and then a stile. After a stile, turn right and follow a path beneath the trees to a stile. Cross this and continue on the same line to come to a road. Turn sharp right and follow a descending track – this was the original road into **Tetbury**. At its end you will emerge to the right of the arched road bridge. Turn left, through the far arch, and then bear right up a path – this brings you up to the centre of Tetbury, with the **church** to the right.

WHAT TO LOOK FOR

Note the **cupola** on the roof of the market hall, containing a bell and surmounted by a weather vane featuring a pair of dolphins. These have come to be adopted as an unofficial coat-of-arms for the town. Nobody, however, has ever been able to explain their origin.

Walk 41

All Saxons and Severn at Deerhurst

An easy walk by the river to discover a rare, complete Saxon chapel on the banks of the Severn.

•DISTANCE•	3¼ miles (5.3km)
•MINIMUM TIME•	1hr 30min
•ASCENT / GRADIENT•	115ft (35m) ▲▲▲
•LEVEL OF DIFFICULTY•	👫 👫 👫
•PATHS•	Fields, pavement and riverbank, 11 stiles
•LANDSCAPE•	Hills, villages and river
•SUGGESTED MAP•	aqua3 OS Explorer 179 Gloucester, Cheltenham & Stroud
•START / FINISH•	Grid reference: SO 868298
•DOG FRIENDLINESS•	Off leads except near occasional livestock
•PARKING•	Car park (small fee) outside Odda's Chapel
•PUBLIC TOILETS•	None on route

BACKGROUND TO THE WALK

Deerhurst, a small, pretty village on the banks of Britain's longest river, the Severn, is endowed with a chapel and a church of particular, if not unique, significance. Both buildings hark back to that poignant period of English history immediately before the Norman Conquest. At the time of their arrival, in the 5th and 6th centuries AD, after the withdrawal of the Romans, the Saxons were a pagan people. But they were gradually converted through the influence of St Augustine and the preaching of the British or Celtic church. Deerhurst was in the Saxon kingdom of Hwicce, an area that was converted to Celtic Christianity by Welsh missionaries.

A Visit to Rome

In AD 800 Aethelric, ruler of Hwicce, was inspired by a visit to Rome – on his return he set aside a large acreage of land at Deerhurst for the construction of a monastery. The monastery became the most important in Hwicce and indeed one of its monks, Alphege, was to become Archbishop of Canterbury in the early 11th century. The monastery, however, was partially destroyed by the Danes in the 9th century. Although a small monastic community stayed on, it was finally levelled at the time of the Dissolution. Nonetheless, the monastery church at Deerhurst, once as important as Gloucester and Tewkesbury, has survived as the finest Saxon church in England. It contains some 30 Anglo-Saxon doors and windows as well as a 9th-century font. The Deerhurst Angel, located outside on the east wall, dates from the 10th century.

Odda's Chapel

A short distance from the church is Odda's Chapel, one of only a handful of wholly Saxon buildings left in England. It takes its name from Earl Odda, a kinsman of Edward the Confessor. When his brother, Aelfric, died at Deerhurst in AD 1053, Odda had this chapel built, to be used as an oratory and to be served by the monastery monks. It owes its survival entirely to chance. The monastery, and the chapel, eventually became the property of Westminster Abbey. The chapel was later deconsecrated and subsumed into the adjoining abbot's house. After the monastery's Dissolution in January 1540 the abbot's house became a farmhouse and the existence of the disused chapel was quite forgotten. It was only in 1885, during restoration work on the house, that the chapel was rediscovered and its significance understood. The building you see today is one of great simplicity – a stone room with high walls and only two windows – but its antiquity, location, and its almost pristine state seem somehow awe-inspiring.

Near by, and also visited on this walk, is the scattered village of Apperley. Here you'll see some very fine, timbered houses, one of which is the post office. The Coalhouse Inn, on the riverbank, was built in the 18th century to cater for the bargees who were transporting coal from the Forest of Dean up-river to Gloucester and Tewkesbury.

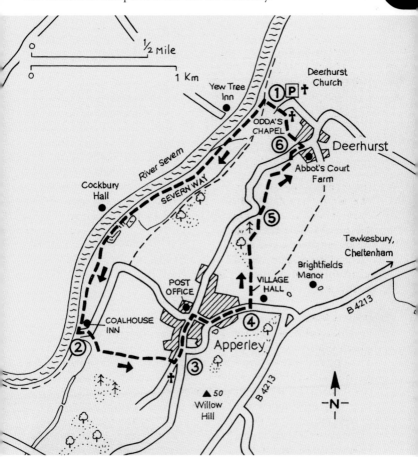

Walk 41 Directions

① With **Odda's Chapel** behind you, turn left and then right through a gate to walk along a track

as far as the riverbank. Here, turn left to follow the **Severn Way**. Continue through a number of gates and over stiles, following an obvious path (sometimes a little overgrown), with the river always

Walk 41

close by on the right. Eventually you reach the **Coalhouse Inn**, set back a little to the left.

② Turn left after the pub to follow a road. Once behind the pub turn right through a kissing gate on to an area of rough grass. Go half right to a stile and cross into a field. Continue to another stile. In the following field go uphill to find another stile at the top, beside a gate. Go over and follow the right-hand margin of the field to another gate. Go through, and continue to the road in **Apperley**.

WHERE TO EAT AND DRINK ⓘ

During the walk you will pass the **Coalhouse Inn**, prettily situated on the riverbank near Apperley. The post office in the village also sells snacks, ice creams and drinks. Otherwise, there is the **Swan** at Coombe Hill, towards Cheltenham. Here you'll find a bar and restaurant menu and several real ales.

---

③ Turn left to walk through the village. Opposite the **post office** (which will be on your left) turn right down a road with houses on your left.

④ Just before the **village hall** turn left and walk across the playing fields to a stile. Cross and stay on the same line to arrive at another stile. Now follow the right-hand margin of a field as it eventually curves right and brings you to a stile at a lane.

⑤ Go over to the lane and turn sharp right to a gate. Once in the field turn left to come swiftly to another stile. Cross this to enter another field and then walk down,

---

WHILE YOU'RE THERE ⓘ

Tewkesbury, the neighbouring town just north of Deerhurst, is certainly worth a visit. The Abbey church is one of the most magnificent in the country, its massive Norman tower the largest in Europe. The town has many literary and historical associations (► Walk 35).

---

crossing another stile and passing to the right of a house. Cross another stile (if there is one – it may be a temporary measure) and go half left to a stile in the hedge, well before a farm in front of you. Go over to a road and turn right.

⑥ Continue until you come to a concrete block on your left. Go up this and walk along a ridge alongside a private garden. Cross a stile into a meadow and continue diagonally right heading for a stile and gate beside **Odda's Chapel** and the timbered building next to it. This will bring you to a gate by your starting point.

WHAT TO LOOK FOR ⓘ

This part of the River Severn is much used by **river craft** of all sorts (although commercial traffic has completely disappeared). Look out for sailing craft from the sailing club on the far bank, rowing boats and, sometimes, beautifully painted longboats that have been rented by holiday makers.

Severnside at Ashleworth and Hasfield

A fine walk along the banks of the River Severn, visiting a huge, and beautifully-preserved, tithe barn.

•DISTANCE•	7 miles (11.3km)
•MINIMUM TIME•	3hrs 15min
•ASCENT / GRADIENT•	65ft (20m)
•LEVEL OF DIFFICULTY•	
•PATHS•	Tracks, fields, lanes and riverbank, 16 stiles
•LANDSCAPE•	Flat: river, meadows, woods, farms, villages and distant hills
•SUGGESTED MAP•	aqua3 OS Explorer 179 Gloucester, Cheltenham & Stroud
•START / FINISH•	Grid reference: SO 818251
•DOG FRIENDLINESS•	Not much livestock but many stiles
•PARKING•	Grass verges in vicinity of tithe barn
•PUBLIC TOILETS•	None on route

BACKGROUND TO THE WALK

Medieval tithe barns, such as the impressive example at Ashleworth, still survive around the country in surprisingly large numbers. In many cases they are still in use, even if the original purpose for which they were built has long been an irrelevance. They date back to the period before the 16th century, when the great monasteries owned much of the land that was not held by the Crown. Around Ashleworth the land belonged to Bristol Abbey. The local people who worked the land were their tenants. There were different categories of tenant who, in return for working the land of their landlord, were allowed access to common land and also to work a certain amount of land for themselves.

Medieval Taxes

Whatever category they belonged to, they all shared one special obligation and that was the payment of tithes, or taxes, to the abbey. This was most often in the form of produce, stored in the tithe barn, which usually stood close to the church and the abbot's residence. If the abbot was not in permanent residence then he would make regular visits with his entourage to ensure that the tithes were paid correctly and on time. The presence of a huge tithe barn here, in what today is a comparatively remote village, has a geographical explanation. Ashleworth is situated at an easily fordable part of the river – an important consideration before the era of easy transportation. There had been a church at Ashleworth since before the compilation of the Domesday Book. A manor house certainly existed during the Norman period, and no doubt before. The barn, and Ashleworth Court next to it (which was used as an administrative centre), date from the late 15th century.

Kings and Queens

The limestone barn is 125ft (38m) long, consisting of ten bays – this is an enormous building by any standards. If you look up to the stone slate roof you can only marvel at the deceptively simple timber braces that support it. In this barn 'queen post trusses' are used, that is, a trellis of posts standing vertically from the horizontal tie beams, as opposed to a 'king post truss', consisting of a single vertical post. The bays would have been used to store both tithes and also the normal produce of the farm. Had you wandered through the barn 500 years ago you would have seen different types of grain, honey, dairy produce and, of course, Cotswold wool, all of which would have been subsequently shipped downriver. Ashleworth Court, next door, is a fine example of a medieval stone building barely changed since the time of its construction. The black and white, timbered Manor House, built as the abbot's residence, stands a short distance along the road.

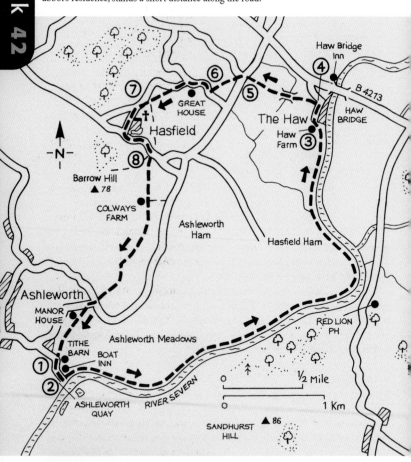

Walk 42 Directions

① From the **tithe barn** walk along the road towards the **River Severn**, passing the **Boat Inn** on your left-hand side.

② Turn left over a stile to walk along the riverbank. Follow it for a little over 3 miles (4.8km). In general the path is obvious, but where it sometimes appears to pass through gates, you may find that they are locked and that you should instead be using a stile closer to the river. **Sandhurst Hill** will come and go across the river, followed by the **Red Lion** pub (sadly also out of reach across the river).

③ Eventually you will pass a house. Immediately after it follow a track that leads left, away from the river, and then passes to the left of a number of houses and cottages. The track becomes a lane and the **Haw Bridge** will appear before you.

WHILE YOU'RE THERE　ⓘ

Visit **Gloucester**, a city whose beauty it is still possible to discern, notwithstanding years of unsympathetic development. Gloucester Cathedral is of enormous historical and architectural interest, whilst the old docks, though no longer commercially operational, have been rescued from oblivion – the former warehouses have been turned into museums and shops.

④ Just before the lane goes left turn left over a stile into a field. Walk straight on and then, as the field opens up at a corner, bear half left to arrive at a stile. In the the next field, after a few paces, turn right to cross a bridge. Continue straight on across two fields.

WHAT TO LOOK FOR　ⓘ

The **River Severn** can flood quite badly and you will notice a number of damage limitation devices built in the vicinity of Ashleworth and elsewhere. In the past floods have reached as far as the church every two or three years. The worst flood, however, was in 1947. The level the water reached is recorded on the wall of the south aisle.

---

⑤ This will bring you to a lane. Cross it to walk down the road opposite and then, after about 150yds (46m), look for a bridge and stile concealed in the hedge on the left. Cross to a field and aim half right to a gateway in a hedge. Continue on the same line in the next field and pass through a gateway in the corner to a road.

⑥ Turn right and pass the **Great House**. Stay on the lane as it bears left. Then, after passing two houses, cross left into a field. Head downhill, half right, to a corner and rejoin the lane.

⑦ Turn left and continue into **Hasfield**, keeping left for **Ashleworth**. Turn left to visit the church and return to carry on through the village, still heading towards Ashleworth.

⑧ Before a row of cottages on the right, turn right at a footpath sign. Where the path divides, take the far left one across several fields on the same line, passing left of **Colways Farm**. This will bring you to a lane opposite the turning for **Ashleworth Quay**. Just left of the road opposite is a stile leading into a field. Go over and head across to another stile. Now follow the path on the right side of fields all the way back to a point just before the **tithe barn**.

WHERE TO EAT AND DRINK　ⓘ

Early on the route, beside the river at Ashleworth Quay, is the **Boat Inn**, an exceptionally unpretentious and comfortable pub. There is also a pub just off the route on the other side of the B4213 at Haw Bridge (unsurprisingly the **Haw Bridge Inn**).

Uley and its Magnificent Fort on the Hill

The vast bulk of the ancient fort of Uley Bury forms the centrepiece for this walk along the Cotswold escarpment.

•DISTANCE•	3 miles (4.8km)
•MINIMUM TIME•	1hr 30min
•ASCENT / GRADIENT•	345ft (105m) ▲▲▲
•LEVEL OF DIFFICULTY•	🚶 🚶 🚶
•PATHS•	Tracks and fields
•LANDSCAPE•	Valley, meadows, woodland and open hilltop
•SUGGESTED MAP•	aqua3 OS Explorer 168 Stroud, Tetbury and Malmesbury
•START / FINISH•	Grid reference: ST 789984
•DOG FRIENDLINESS•	Good – little or no livestock, few stiles
•PARKING•	Main street of Uley
•PUBLIC TOILETS•	None on route

BACKGROUND TO THE WALK

Uley is a pretty village, strung along a wide street at the foot of a high, steep hill. It is distinctive for several reasons. It has its own brewery, which produces some fine beers including Uley Bitter and Uley Old Spot. In the past the village specialised in the production of 'Uley Blue' cloth, which was used in military uniforms. And then there is Uley Bury, dating back to the Iron Age and one of the finest hill forts in the Cotswolds.

Peaceful Settlements
There are many hundreds of Iron-Age forts throughout England and Wales. They are concentrated in Cornwall, south west Wales and the Welsh Marches, with secondary concentrations throughout the Cotswolds, North Wales and Wessex. Although the term 'hill fort' is generally used in connection with these settlements, the term can be misleading. There are many that were built on level ground and there are many that were not used purely for military purposes – often they were simply settlements located on easily-defended sites. Broadly speaking, there are five types, classified according to the nature of the site on which they were built, rather than, say, the date of their construction.

Contour forts were built more or less along the perimeter edge of a hilltop; promontory forts were built on a spur, surrounded by natural defences on two or more sides; valley and plateau forts (two types) depended heavily on artificial defences and were located, as their names suggest, in valleys or on flat land respectively; and multiple-enclosure forts were usually built in a poor strategic position on the slope of a hill and were perhaps used as stockades.

Natural Defences
Uley Bury, covering about 38 acres (15.4ha), is classified as an inland promontory fort and was built in the 6th century BC. It falls away on three sides, the fourth side, which faces away from the escarpment, is protected by specially constructed ramparts which would have

been surmounted by a wooden palisade. The natural defences – that is, the Cotswold escarpment, facing west – were also strengthened by the construction of a wide and deep ditch, as well as two additional ramparts, an inner one and an outer one, between which the footpath largely threads its course. The three main entrances were at the northern, eastern and southern corners. These, being the most vulnerable parts of the fort, would have been fortified with massive log barriers.

Although some tribespeople would have lived permanently in huts within the fort, most would have lived outside, either on other parts of the hill or in the valleys below. In an emergency, therefore, there was space for those who lived outside the fort to take shelter within. Eventually the fort was taken over by the Dobunni tribe – Celtic interlopers from mainland Europe who arrived about 100 BC – and appears to have been occupied by them throughout the Roman era.

Walk 43

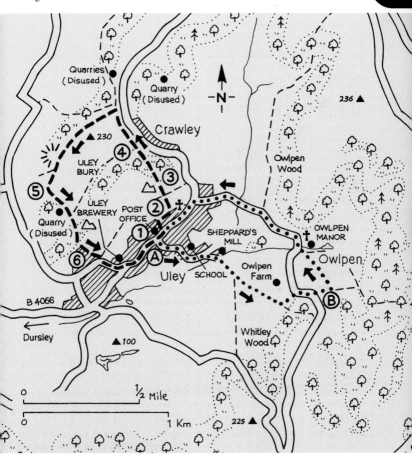

Walk 43 Directions

① From the main street locate the **post office** (on your left as you walk up the street). Walk along the

narrow lane (to the right, as you look at it). Pass between houses as the lane dwindles to a track. Immediately before a stile turn right along an enclosed path towards the **church**.

② When the churchyard can be seen on the right, turn left up a narrow path beside a cottage. This rises fairly sharply and brings you to a kissing gate. Pass through into a meadow. Climb steeply up the grassland towards woodland.

③ At the tree-line keep left of the woods. In a corner go through a gate and follow a winding woodland path, climbing among the trees. When you come to a fence stay on the path as it bears left. Go over a stile and then continue ascending, to emerge from the woods. Stay on the path as it rises across grassland to a junction.

WHERE TO EAT AND DRINK ⓘ

The **Old Crown** on the main street opposite the church in Uley is a very picturesque village local, with lots of memorabilia on the wallls, exposed beams and a small, sunny garden. Beers come from the local brewery and include Uley Bitter and Uley Old Spot, named after the Gloucestershire pigs.

---

④ Turn right to follow the contour of the hill – the edge of the ancient fort. You are following the perimeter of the fort in an anti-clockwise direction, with steep drops to your right. When you meet

---

WHAT TO LOOK FOR ⓘ

There are **magnificent views** westward from the summit of Uley Bury. You should easily be able to see the estuary of the River Severn, as well as the Tyndale Monument. Look out too for the **brewery** in Uley and the statue of a pig outside it. This is a Gloucester Old Spot, a breed of pig peculiar to the county, now making something of a comeback.

---

another junction of paths go left along the edge of the hill, with views to the west.

⑤ At the next corner continue to follow the edge of the fort, disregarding a stile that invites you to descend. At the next corner, at the fort's south eastern point, bear right on a path that descends through hillocks and then quite steeply through bushes, keeping left. This will bring you to a stile into a meadow and a tarmac path.

⑥ Walk along the path, all the way to a cottage and then a kissing gate. Go through this and pass beside the cottage to arrive at a lane. Turn left here and follow the lane, soon passing the **Uley Brewery**, to reach the main road. Turn left, passing **South Street** (Point Ⓐ on Walk 44), to return to the start.

WHILE YOU'RE THERE ⓘ

Two sites are worth a closer look while you're in the area. Near by is the little village of North Nibley, over which towers the 111ft (34m) **Tyndale Monument**. Built in 1866 this is a tribute to William Tyndale (c1494–1536). He was born at Dursley near Gloucester, and was the first to translate the New Testament of the Bible from Latin into English. It is possible to climb to near the top of the tower for maginificent views. Just to the north of Uley Bury, and still on the escarpment, is Uley Long Barrow, better known as **Hetty Pegler's Tump**. This is a neolithic chambered tomb some 180ft (55m) in length. A narrow stone doorway leads into a passage, off which four semicircular chambers would have contained cremated remains.

Over the Fields to Owlpen Manor

Extend Walk 43 to the other side of this idyllic valley to see a picturesque manor house.
See map and information panel for Walk 43

•DISTANCE•	5 miles (8km)
•MINIMUM TIME•	2hrs 15min
•ASCENT / GRADIENT•	115ft (35m)
•LEVEL OF DIFFICULTY•	

Walk 44 Directions (Walk 43 option)

From Point Ⓐ turn right to walk along **South Street**. Follow the road as it goes left and passes the school. Keep going until it forks, at which point go right, heading for **Sheppard's Mill**. Keep to the right of the mill (now converted to a private dwelling) and come to a stile. Cross this and continue ahead to a gate. Proceed to a stile and then uphill to another. Cross it and turn sharp left, with houses to the left, and walk ahead until you reach a stile at a road.

Cross the stile and turn right uphill for 100yds (91m). Just before a house, turn left through a gate into a field. Go half right, looking for a gate ahead of you at a protuberant corner of a fence, Point Ⓑ. Pass through into the next field and then go half left, aiming for a point to the left of the church you can see below you, just to the left of **Owlpen Manor**. Keep going to the far side of the field, from where you will have a fine view of the manor house.

This is an impossibly idyllic scene. To your left, the broad valley sweeps grandly southwards, its sides covered densely in trees, with the village of Uley asleep at the feet of the fortified hill. Before you is a picturesque, 15th-century manor house (with additions from later centuries), bedded into a green hollow. In fact, the foundations of the house are far earlier, dating back to 1080. The house was restored in the 1920s by Norman Jewson, an influential member of the Arts and Crafts movement in Daneway and Sapperton (► Walk 33). The house's charming name is actually a corruption of 'de Olepennes', the family that owned the manor until 1490. The Victorian church has a colourful interior, and a number of brasses commemorating members of the Daunt family, who succeded the de Olepennes as lords of the manor, remaining until 1805.

Locate a stile in the corner and drop down to a lane. Turn right, pass the entrance to the church (which can be visited by following signs), and follow the lane all the way back to **Uley** to emerge high up the main street. Turn left to return to the post office.

Little Sodbury's Fort and Horton Court

Encountering the ancient and the medieval along a new way.

•DISTANCE•	3¾ miles (6km)
•MINIMUM TIME•	1hr 45min
•ASCENT / GRADIENT•	245ft (75m) ▲▲ ▲ ▲
•LEVEL OF DIFFICULTY•	🚶 🚶 🚶
•PATHS•	Tracks, fields, woodland and lanes, 9 stiles
•LANDSCAPE•	Meadows and open hilltop
•SUGGESTED MAP•	aqua3 OS Explorer 167 Thornbury, Dursley & Yate
•START / FINISH•	Grid reference: ST 759844
•DOG FRIENDLINESS•	Livestock in initial fields, thereafter reasonably good
•PARKING•	Horton village
•PUBLIC TOILETS•	None on route

Walk 45 Directions

Walk up the hill out of Horton. Near the top turn right on to a track towards **Little Sodbury**. After 20yds (18m), go left through a fence to a path. Continue to a stile, to follow the **Cotswold Way**, marked by a white dot or an acorn.

Nearly 50 years have elapsed since the notion of a continuous route through the Cotswolds was born. The Cotswold Way will be 'officially' opened in 2004. In preparation for this, improvements to the waymarking and other facilities

have been undertaken. Among these is the ongoing replacement of the 'white dot' – the route's distinguishing mark throughout its time as a regional route – with the 'acorn' that signifies its status as an official National Trail.

Cross the field in front of you and come to a stile on the far side. Descend a steep bank in a field and continue across it, on the same line, to another stile. Walk across the following field, with a hedge to your right, to a stile in the corner. Cross on to a path beside a cottage and turn left to follow a path to a lane in **Little Sodbury**. Turn right and, at the next junction, left. Pass **Little Sodbury church** on your left and continue along this lane for 550yds (503m). At a junction, fork left along what is really the drive to **Little Sodbury Manor**. After a few paces turn right on to a path, then, at the next corner, bear left as the path rises up the slope and brings you to the fortified-looking walls of a farmhouse. To visit **Little**

Walk 45

Sodbury hill fort, turn right and then left through a kissing gate. The fort is considered to be one of the finest in the Cotswolds, (▶ Background to Walk 43).

Turn left and, at the end of the wall, turn right through a gate. Turn left to pass a shed and then cross a paddock to a gate. Go through to a field and cross half right to a ladder stile. Go over to a lane and cross to enter another lane in front of you. Follow this for 700yds (640m), until you come to a junction. Turn right. Follow the road for about 50yds (46m) then, at a corner, leave the road to enter a lane. Follow this for 750yds (686m), passing **Top Farm** to your left. Turn left on to a path through woodland. Follow this to the end to a stile at a field. Cross to another stile at a lane and turn right. Walk down the lane, passing the entrance to **Horton Court**.

Founded in 1140, Horton Court is one of the oldest inhabited buildings in the Cotswolds, and probably the oldest rectory in England. The original limestone house was little more than a single great hall, which still survives, although the house was greatly embellished and extended under the ownership of William Knight in the 16th century. He was both Bishop of Bath and Wells and Chamberlain to King Henry VIII at the time when the King was seeking to divorce Catherine of Aragon. In fact Henry attempted to send him on a mission to persuade the Pope to allow the divorce, but the plan was scuppered after it was discovered by Cardinal Wolseley.

Horton Court is just one of several historically important sites and landmarks encountered on the Cotswold Way. In total the Way runs for just under 100 miles (161km), keeping close to the Cotswold escarpment, between Chipping Campden in the north and Bath in the south. A route along the Cotswold edge was first mooted in the early 1950s but only in 1968, when Gloucestershire County Council carried out a recreational survey, was the idea resurrected. In 1970 it was decided to create the Cotswold Way, based on existing roads and public rights of way. Amendments were made over the following years, with enthusiastic voluntary help from the Cotswold Warden Service. In 1983 the first official application for national status was made. It took another 15 years before the go-ahead was finally given, and, along with it, entitlement to grant aid for its creation and maintenance.

At the next corner turn sharp left to a bridleway. Cross a field, then pass through a hedge to reach gate. Continue to another gate and then follow a hedge to a stile. Go over to the corner of a protruding hedge and then on to a stile near some houses. Cross this and follow the path back into **Horton**.

Seeking the Severn Bore at Arlingham

A long but fairly level walk along the river where Britain's regular tidal wave rushes in.

•DISTANCE•	7½ miles (12.1km)
•MINIMUM TIME•	3hrs 30min
•ASCENT / GRADIENT•	85ft (25m) ▲▲ ▲ ▲
•LEVEL OF DIFFICULTY•	🚶 🚶 🚶
•PATHS•	Tracks, fields and lanes, 15 stiles
•LANDSCAPE•	River, meadows and distant hills
•SUGGESTED MAP•	aqua3 OS Outdoor Leisure 14 Wye Valley & Forest of Dean
•START / FINISH•	Grid reference: ST 708109
•DOG FRIENDLINESS•	Good, despite stiles, some long, empty stretches
•PARKING•	Arlingham village
•PUBLIC TOILETS•	None on route

BACKGROUND TO THE WALK

The River Severn is at its most impressive around Arlingham – in its lower reaches before opening up to the Bristol Channel. Here Gloucestershire juts out into the river to form a large promontory, forcing the river into a huge sweeping loop, widening to well over half a mile (800m) at certain points. To the west it is overlooked by the Forest of Dean ridge, to the east by the Cotswold escarpment.

Bore Formula

Shallow and placid though it might appear here, the River Severn has a capricious nature. The area has been devastated by floods in the past, most notably in the 16th century. The Severn Bore, for which the river is justly famous, is a tidal wave that is formed a little way downstream, where the river narrows at Sharpness. The fundamental cause behind the bore is the combination of a large volume of tidal water, funnelled into a quickly narrowing channel, hastening on to rock rising from the riverbed. A wave is created, which is then free to roll on to the Severn's middle reaches. Flooding, however, is rarely a problem here now, as the flood control measures you see as you walk have succeeded in containing the river. It does, though, continue to create havoc every winter further upstream. Significant sea tides at the river's wide mouth make the Severn Bore such a spectacle. In fortnightly cycles over the course of each month the tides reach their highest and lowest points. Near the Severn Bridge the second highest rise and fall of tide in the world has been recorded (the first is in Canada, on the Petitcodiac River). Once a month, for a few days, the spring tides occur, reaching a height of 31 feet (9.4m) at Sharpness. Whenever the tides reach 26 ft (8m) or more, a bore will be unleashed.

Exciting Boring

Because of its tendency to extremes, the Severn can be a dangerous place. The shallow and placid-seeming stream, that may invite you to paddle on a summer's day, can be transformed almost instantaneously into a swirling current capable of knocking you off your feet and carrying you away. Nonetheless, there are those who love to ride the bore. In the past boatsmen used it as a means of being borne upstream. Now surfers and canoeists ride it for the thrill. It is not something to be undertaken lightly, as the waves will sometimes reach almost 10ft (3m) and travel at 12mph (19kph), finally losing its impetus near Gloucester. Annual tables are produced that predict the best days for seeing the bore but, in truth, much depends on luck.

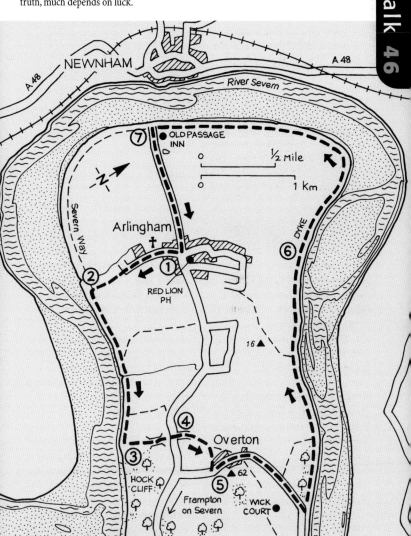

Walk 46 **Directions**

① From the centre of the village, with the **Red Lion** at your back,

walk along a 'No Through Road'. Pass the **church** and stay on the road. It becomes a track which brings you to a stile beneath a bank. Go to the top of the bank.

Walk 46

② With the **River Severn** on your right, turn left over a stile. Continue along this obvious route, crossing stiles where they arise and ignoring any footpaths inviting you inland, until you see **Hock Cliff** in front of you. Cross a stile to enter the field that begins to slope up towards the cliff. (You can continue up to the cliff itself and return to this point if you wish, though the views are hardly stunning.)

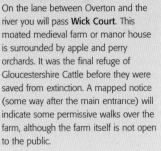

WHILE YOU'RE THERE
On the lane between Overton and the river you will pass **Wick Court**. This moated medieval farm or manor house is surrounded by apple and perry orchards. It was the final refuge of Gloucestershire Cattle before they were saved from extinction. A mapped notice (some way after the main entrance) will indicate some permissive walks over the farm, although the farm itself is not open to the public.

WHAT TO LOOK FOR
Hock Cliff, composed of clay and limestone, is well-known for its fossils, including the so-called Devil's toenails, ammonites, belemnites and many others. Towards the walk's end, approaching the Old Passage Inn, you will see **Newnham** across the river. Tradition has it that the Romans crossed the river here by elephant to attack fugitive Britons.

③ Turn sharp left to walk down the bank and along the left side of a field. Cross a bridge into the next field. Continue to a track and turn left. After some 60yds (55m) turn right over a stile, on to a path running between hedges.

④ Cross a road and enter the 'No Through Road' in front of you. Follow it as it curves right towards some houses. Just before a gateway turn left over a stile into a field. Follow its right-hand side to another stile and then continue forward on the same line. Pass a

WHERE TO EAT AND DRINK
There are two pubs on this route. The **Red Lion** is in the centre of Arlingham and the **Old Passage Inn** (which specialises in fresh fish) is on the riverbank to the west of Arlingham. The nearest towns offering a wider choice are Stroud or Gloucester.

house on your right and then, about 60yds (55m) before some farm buildings, turn right over a stile into a field. Cross this to another stile which takes you out on to a country lane.

⑤ Turn left and follow the lane through **Overton** for just over ½ mile (800m). Where the road goes sharply right beside a long house, turn left over a stile to rejoin the **Severn Way**. Cross several more stiles and the path will lead away from the river briefly, among trees, to emerge at a stile beside a meadow. Continue walking ahead, maintaining your direction, passing through gates and over stiles, always with the River Severn on your right and again ignoring any paths leading inland.

⑥ The footpath will soon take the form of a raised bank, or dyke. It reaches its westernmost point then swings to the south, just after passing a farm – the town of **Newnham** should now be clearly visible on the opposite bank. Continue to a pub, the **Old Passage Inn**, on your left.

⑦ Beyond the pub take the long, straight lane on your left, which leads across the flood plain, all the way back to **Arlingham**.

The Wartime Poets of Dymock

A quiet backwater on the border with Herefordshire was once home to some of the finest poets of the early 20th century.

•DISTANCE•	8 miles (12.9km)
•MINIMUM TIME•	3hrs 45min
•ASCENT / GRADIENT•	100ft (30m) ▲▲ ▲
•LEVEL OF DIFFICULTY•	👫 👫 👫
•PATHS•	Fields and lanes, 27 stiles
•LANDSCAPE•	Woodland, hills, villages, rural farmland and streams
•SUGGESTED MAP•	aqua3 OS Outdoor Leisure 14 Wye Valley & Forest of Dean; Explorers 189 Hereford & Ross-on-Wye; 190 Malvern Hills & Bredon Hill
•START / FINISH•	Grid reference: SO 677288 (on Outdoor Leisure 14)
•DOG FRIENDLINESS•	Stiles and some livestock but plenty of off-lead potential
•PARKING•	Main road of Kempley Green, near its south eastern end
•PUBLIC TOILETS•	None on route

BACKGROUND TO THE WALK

Dymock lies in a frequently overlooked, remote corner of Gloucestershire, on the border with Herefordshire. In the years leading up to the First World War this pretty, unspoilt area became the home and inspiration to a group now known as the Dymock Poets. Some went on to lasting fame, others have been all but forgotten. The first to settle in Dymock, in 1911, was Lascelles Abercrombie. He was followed by Wilfrid Gibson and then by the American poet Robert Frost. Edward Thomas rented a cottage here in 1914 and all played host to John Drinkwater, Rupert Brooke and Eleanor Farjeon. Were it not for the Great War, they may well have continued living and working here, united as they were by a love for the English countryside and a respect for each other's abilities. As it was, their friendship was the catalyst to a considerable body of work, much of which can claim to have been inspired by experiences and friendships gained at Dymock.

Forgotten Talent

Abercrombie lived at a cottage called Gallows, at Ryton, to the east of Dymock. Forgotten though he is, at the beginning of the 20th century he was hailed by the *Times Literary Supplement* as a great talent. It was his move to Dymock that was emulated by Gibson, who settled at the Old Nail Shop in Greenway Cross. Gibson, too, is now unknown, but at the time he was the best-read poet in the country. His move to Dymock led to frequent visits by Brooke and Drinkwater. The four of them contributed to a quarterly called *New Numbers*, published from Ryton in 1914 and which contained some of Brook's poems. Robert Frost, who became involved through a review of his poetry by Abercrombie, rented a cottage called Little Iddens whilst Edward Thomas (who immortalised the Cotswold village of Adlestrop in his most famous poem, ▶ Walk 1) lived in a cottage near by, called Old Fields. It was Frost who persuaded Thomas to concentrate on his poetry rather than his prose.

Dymock and the Daffodil Way

Dymock, which has a number of attractive timber houses, was also the birthplace of John Kyrle, the so-called 'Man of Ross'. A local justice and benefactor to the town of Ross-on-Wye in neighbouring Herefordshire in the late 17th and early 18th century, he acquired his moniker though his countless good deeds. These included securing a spire and bell for the parish church. Kyrle was actually the Earl of Ross by birth, but his good work earned him respect as a common 'man of Ross'.

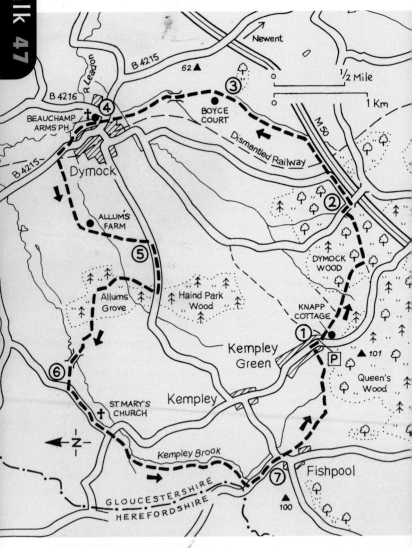

Walk 47 Directions

① Walk south-east out of **Kempley Green** and turn left just before

Knapp Cottage. Take the right-hand of two paths. Cross stiles, pass a barn and then go through a gate into an orchard. Enter **Dymock Wood** to follow a path to a road.

② Turn right and then left before a motorway bridge. Where this road bears left, proceed through a gate into fields and follow the route, alongside the motorway, down to a stream. Turn left before it. Cross a track and stiles, pass through a gate and walk straight along a track, aiming to the right of **Boyce Court**.

③ Pass to the left of a lake and continue through woodland to a lane. Turn right over a bridge and left on to a path beside the stream. Continue on the same line, staying first right and then left of the stream, all the way to **Dymock**.

④ Go into the **churchyard** and out the other side, through a gate into a field. Turn half left and take the second bridge on the right. Then bear half left to a stile. Turn right along a disused road and cross the **B4215**. Follow a track, leaving it to keep to the right of **Allum's Farm**. Pass a barn and go half left across the field to a gate. Enter an orchard, turn right and follow its left margin and then that of a field, to a road.

⑤ Turn right. After 600yds (549m) turn right into a field alongside woodland. After 120yds (110m) go half right over a mound to enter the woods. Turn right and follow the boundary to a stile. Turn left and re-enter woodland. Follow an obvious path, eventually emerging at a stile. Cross a field, keeping to the left of a chimney, and then right into a field. Look for a stile on your

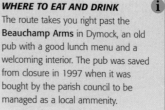

> **WHERE TO EAT AND DRINK** ⓘ
> The route takes you right past the **Beauchamp Arms** in Dymock, an old pub with a good lunch menu and a welcoming interior. The pub was saved from closure in 1997 when it was bought by the parish council to be managed as a local ammenity.

left, cross into the adjacent field and then turn right to find a bridge across the stream. Go half left across fields to a road.

⑥ Turn left and carry on past **St Mary's Church**. At the next T-junction go into the field ahead. Proceed into the next field and continue with the stream on your left across several fields to a lane. Turn left to a junction at **Fishpool**.

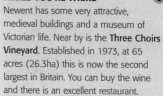

> **WHILE YOU'RE THERE** ⓘ
> Newent has some very attractive, medieval buildings and a museum of Victorian life. Near by is the **Three Choirs Vineyard**. Established in 1973, at 65 acres (26.3ha) this is now the second largest in Britain. You can buy the wine and there is an excellent restaurant.

⑦ Turn right and, after 50yds (46m), turn left over a stile. Curve right and then pass a series of stiles to aim eventually just to the right of a cottage. Follow the path through poultry enclosures and then bear left over stiles so that a house is on your right. Pass the house and go right into a field. Turn left and follow the same line to arrive at **Kempley Green**.

> **WHAT TO LOOK FOR** ⓘ
> The isolated **St Mary's Church**, which was once the parish church of Kempley, contains some fine 14th-century mural fragments depicting a wheel of life and St Michael weighing souls. The chancel contains the most complete set of Romanesque wall paintings in England. Completed between 1132 and 1140, they had been painted over and were not rediscovered until 1872. They show Christ in Benediction, the Apostles, pilgrims and the usual members of the sacred host.

Along Offa's Dyke

Exploring the Saxon King's earthwork along the Celtic border.

•DISTANCE•	4½ miles (7.2km)
•MINIMUM TIME•	2hrs 15min
•ASCENT / GRADIENT•	740ft (225m) ▲▲▲
•LEVEL OF DIFFICULTY•	👫 👫 👫
•PATHS•	Tracks, fields, lanes, stony paths and riverbank; 5 stiles
•LANDSCAPE•	River, meadows, woodland, farmland and village
•SUGGESTED MAP•	aqua3 OS Outdoor Leisure 14 Wye Valley & Forest of Dean
•START / FINISH•	Grid reference: ST 540011
•DOG FRIENDLINESS•	Off lead for long stretches, but occasional livestock
•PARKING•	Lay-by near telephone box in Brockweir or Tintern Old Railway Station, on other side of river (fee)
•PUBLIC TOILETS•	None on route (except at Tintern Old Railway Station)

BACKGROUND TO THE WALK

Offa's Dyke is a massive earthwork constructed by King Offa, the ruler of the Saxon kingdom of Mercia, in the 8th century AD. The dyke represented the western frontier of his kingdom and ran for about 170 miles (274km) from Chepstow in the south (near the confluence of the Wye and the Severn) to Prestatyn in the north. Its basic construction consisted of a bank of earth, 20ft (6.1m) high and 8ft (2.4m) wide, with a ditch at the foot of its western flank. Even today the frontier between Wales and England runs largely along the course of the dyke. (On this stretch the River Wye forms the present-day boundary between Gloucestershire and Monmouthshire.) The construction of the dyke was felt to be necessary because, after the Romans decamped and the Angles and Saxons invaded, Britain was divided into a number of warring kingdoms. Among these Mercia finally became pre-eminent in England, but the Celtic Britons clung tenaciously to their western mountains. Under Offa, Mercia gradually absorbed other Saxon kingdoms and its King became *de facto* ruler of the English in England.

Definitive Boundary
It is not thought that the dyke was conceived as a fortification – it was more a means of definitively marking the boundary between Mercia and its neighbouring kingdoms. Nor was it the first of its kind. Other Saxon rulers had defined their kingdoms in a similar fashion, but none had done so on the scale undertaken by Offa. There is some variation in build quality throughout its length, but it is nonetheless an impressive achievement for its time. The Offa's Dyke Path, opened in 1971, is more or less the same length as the dyke itself but only rarely do the two coincide precisely.

Brockweir was once the most important port of the River Wye. Together with the River Severn, the River Wye was the main trade route serving the Forest of Dean. Timber, iron and coal from the Forest were brought to Brockweir, loaded at the wharf and shipped downstream to Chepstow. A horse-drawn tram that brought the goods from the mines also served the port. Brockweir was also a centre of shipbuilding. All of this came to an end with the arrival of the railway in the late 19th century.

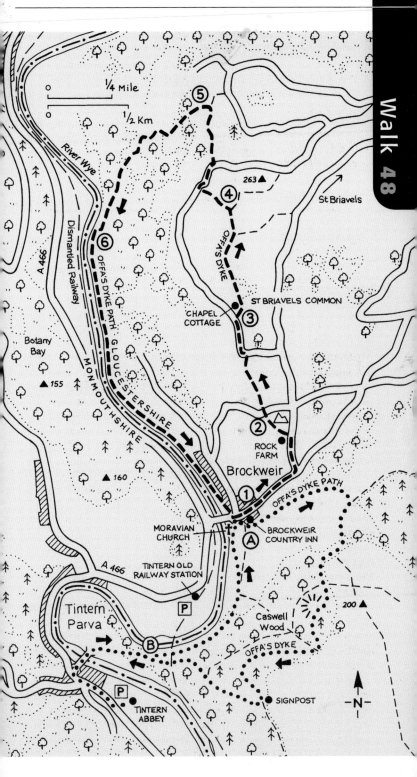

Walk 48 Directions

① Walk uphill out of Brockweir until you reach a junction on your left, signposted '**Coldharbour**'. Turn left along this narrow lane for about 160yds (146m). At a corner beside **Rock Farm** turn left on to a track, marked '**Offa's Dyke Path**', which soon narrows markedly and climbs fairly steeply. Keep going up to a lane.

WHERE TO EAT AND DRINK ⓘ

In Brockweir itself is the pretty **Brockweir Country Inn**. Over the bridge and a short distance downstream is **Tintern Old Railway Station**, where a café is open throughout the summer months.

---

② Cross this and continue your ascent until you reach another lane. Turn left here and follow the lane for 200yds (183m), to pass a cottage on the right, followed by some ruined stone buildings. Turn right along a lane.

③ Keep to the right of **Chapel Cottage** on to a path, still ascending. When you reach a wider track, fork left. This dwindles to a path, continuing to climb, until it brings you to another track, beside a stone stile. Turn left again.

④ After a few paces, before a gate and a house, fork right to a stile at a field. Cross this to another pair of stiles, to the left of a house. In the

---

WHAT TO LOOK FOR ⓘ

Near the bridge in **Brockweir** you will probably notice that the water swirls and ruffles for no obvious reason Look more closely and you will see that beneath the water are the remains of the old wharf that was used by trading vessels until the late 19th century.

---

next field stay to the left of a farm and come to a stile at a lane. Turn right and follow this gently climbing lane. It levels out and then, where it starts to climb again at a corner, turn left on to the right-hand path, heading towards Oak Cottage, Bigs Weir and Monmouth. Descend until you arrive at a lane before a house.

⑤ Turn left here to follow a track that descends to the right of another house. This track will continue down into woodland. Stay on the main, obvious track, watching out for loose stones, as it meanders down the hillside. This will bring you to a cottage at a corner. Go left with the track, which later becomes a narrow path. Stay on this and follow it down the side of the hill among trees, still keeping an eye on loose pebbles. Soon the River Wye will appear below you, to the right. At the bottom pass through a gap in the fence, and bear right towards the grassy riverbank, where you will meet a stile.

WHILE YOU'RE THERE ⓘ

In the village of St Briavels is **St Briavel's Castle**. This was built in 1131 by the Earl of Hereford as a centre of administration for the Forest of Dean and the Wye Valley. The castle is not a typical Norman construction as it was never intended as a front-line defensive structure. King John enlarged it in the 13th century and it is now a youth hostel.

---

⑥ Turn left through the stile and follow the river all the way back to Brockweir, passing through gates and crossing bridges where they arise. As you approach the village keep close to the river to enter a path that will bring you on to a lane leading up to the road (Point Ⓐ) at **Brockweir Bridge**.

Tintern Abbey

Extend the walk up to Offa's Dyke and on to Tintern Abbey.
See map and information panel for Walk 48

•DISTANCE•	3 miles (4.8km)
•MINIMUM TIME•	2hrs
•ASCENT / GRADIENT•	740ft (225m) ▲▲▲
•LEVEL OF DIFFICULTY•	🚶🚶 🚶 🚶

Walk 49 Directions
(Walk 48 option)

From Point Ⓐ turn left into Brockweir. Turn right by the **Brockweir Country Inn**. Keep to the right of the farm and after 50yds (46m) turn left, with farm buildings to your left. Climb up this track, passing through gates where they arise. Enter a field and the path bears right, drawing level with a ruined barn. Enter the enclosed path in front of you, running to the right of a field. Follow this to the stile beside a gate at the top. Turn right and, after a few paces, go left up the slope, following markers, to the base of a bank. Turn left at the marker and then right to ascend the bank. At the top of **Offa's Dyke** turn right, following a clear path through woodland.

Pass any stiles that arise and cross any tracks. The path at one point will take you to the edge of the woods with a field to your left. About 600yds (549m) after that you come to another junction. In front of you, although the path continues to the **Devil's Pulpit** (a look-out point), you should turn right at the signpost to follow a stony track towards **Tintern Parva**.

The ruined abbey, founded in 1131, and immortalised in the poem *Tintern Abbey* by William Wordsworth, belonged to the Cistercian order. What is left is the defiantly noble shell of the abbey church, built in English Gothic style between 1270 and 1325. The abbey was 'dissolved' in 1537.

The path is quite clear, bringing you to an obvious track. Turn right and, after just a few paces, turn left on to a footpath descending through woodland. When this meets another footpath at a T-junction turn right, continuing to a track and a stone parapet, Point Ⓑ. To visit **Tintern Abbey**, turn left here, following the track out of the woods to a bridge, crossing over the River Wye into Wales and turning left. Otherwise, turn right here, along the track in the direction of **Brockweir**.

After 700yds (640m) turn left over a stile to the riverbank. Cross to the riverside and turn right to continue to a stile at the **Moravian church** at Brockweir. The Moravian Church, which has its origins in what is now a region of the Czech Republic, is a free church whose precepts influenced John Wesley, creator of the Methodist Church. Pass to the right of the church and then left by the pub to return Point Ⓐ.

Staunton's Stones

A walk amongst massive stones within the woods of the Forest of Dean.

•DISTANCE•	6¼ miles (10.1km)
•MINIMUM TIME•	3hrs
•ASCENT / GRADIENT•	655ft (200m) ▲▲▲
•LEVEL OF DIFFICULTY•	🚶🚶 🚶🚶 🚶🚶
•PATHS•	Forest tracks and paths, 2 stiles
•LANDSCAPE•	Woodland, hills and village
•SUGGESTED MAP•	aqua3 OS Outdoor Leisure 14 Wye Valley & Forest of Dean
•START / FINISH•	Grid reference: SO 539124
•DOG FRIENDLINESS•	Very good
•PARKING•	Parking area down slip road at edge of forest, just before large lay-by (which could also be used)
•PUBLIC TOILETS•	None on route

Walk 50 **Directions**

From the parking area head along a track into the woods. Where the track goes sharply left, turn right on to another track. Follow this for just under ¾ mile (1.2km), until you see large boulders on your right. Turn right to follow a waymarked path up the slope passing first the **Suck Stone** and then, at the top, the **Hearkening Rock**.

These are just two of the many giant stones that you will pass on this walk. Composed of a quartz conglomerate – a mixture of quartz and Old Red Sandstone – they have mostly been formed by natural weathering over millions of years.

WHAT TO LOOK FOR ⓘ

In the village of Staunton look out for the curious **round enclosure** on your left as you pass through the village. This is the village pound where animals were kept before being sent to market, and where strays were secured for their owners to collect them on paying a fine.

The Suck Stone is thought to be one of the largest single boulders in the country with estimates of its weight varying from 4,000 to 14,000 tons. From the Hearkening Rock, keen-eared listeners are supposed to be able to hear messages whispered from the Buckstone (seen later on the walk).

Go up behind the **Hearkening Rock** and, with your back to it, follow a path through the trees to a forest track. Turn left and immediately right, on to a path back into woodland. Stay on this until you come to a T-junction. Turn left and go right at a fork to continue to a forest track. Cross this to enter **Lady Park Nature Reserve**. Creation of the nature reserve is not the first incidence of 'conservation' in the Forest's history. Back in 1668 depletion of the trees prompted a Dean Forest Reforestation Act.

The Forest of Dean is all that remains of the many thousands of acres of woodland that sprouted at the end of the Ice Age. Clearance